PRAYER
AND
PLANNING
FOR THE
Big Day

JILL KELLY & ERIN KELLY-BEAN

PRAYER
AND
PLANNING
FOR THE
Big Day

THE ESSENTIAL WEDDING GUIDE
FOR A BRIDE AND HER MOTHER

WORTHY®
PUBLISHING

Copyright © 2018 by Jill Kelly and Erin Kelly-Bean

Published by Worthy Books, an imprint of Worthy Publishing Group, a division of Worthy Media, Inc., One Franklin Park, 6100 Tower Circle, Suite 210, Franklin, TN 37067. WORTHY is a registered trademark of Worthy Media, Inc.

Helping people experience the heart of God.

Library of Congress Cataloging-in-Publication Data

Names: Kelly, Jill, 1969- author.
Title: Prayer and planning for the big day : the essential wedding guide for a bride and her mother / Jill Kelly and Erin Kelly.
Description: Franklin, TN : Worthy Publishing, 2018. | Includes index.
Identifiers: LCCN 2018038913 | ISBN 9781683972587 (hardcover)
Subjects: LCSH: Christian women—Prayers and devotions. | Brides—Prayers and devotions. | Weddings—Planning.
Classification: LCC BV4844 .K45 2018 | DDC 265/.5—dc23
LC record available at https://lccn.loc.gov/2018038913

Unless otherwise noted all Scripture references are from the Holy Bible, New International Version®, niv®. Copyright © 1973, 1978, 1984, 2011 by Biblica, Inc.® All rights reserved worldwide. | Scripture quotations marked esv are taken from The Holy Bible, English Standard Version. ESV® Text Edition: 2016. Copyright © 2001 by Crossway Bibles, a publishing ministry of Good News Publishers. | Scripture quotations marked gnt are taken from the Good News Translation of the Bible. Copyright © 1992 by American Bible Society. | Scripture quotations marked hcsb are taken from the Holman Christian Standard Bible. Copyright © 1999, 2000, 2002, 2003, 2009 by Holman Bible Publishers, Nashville Tennessee. All rights reserved. | Scripture references marked msg are taken from The Message. Copyright © 1993, 1994, 1995, 1996, 2000, 2001, 2002 by Eugene H. Peterson. | Scripture quotations marked nlt are taken from the Holy Bible, New Living Translation, copyright © 1996, 2004, 2015 by Tyndale House Foundation. Used by permission of Tyndale House Publishers, Inc., Carol Stream, Illinois 60188. All rights reserved.

No part of this publication may be reproduced, stored in a retrieval system, or transmitted in any form or by any means—electronic, mechanical, photocopy, recording, or any other—except for brief quotations in printed reviews, without the prior permission of the publisher.

Published in association with Jana Burson of The Christopher Ferebee Agency, ChristopherFerebee.com.

ISBN: 978-1-68397-258-7

Cover Design: Tim Green, Faceout Studio | faceoutstudio.com
Interior Design: Bart Dawson

Printed in the United States of America

18 19 20 21 22 LSC 10 9 8 7 6 5 4 3 2 1

This book is dedicated to Camryn Kelly, Faith Kelly,
and Paige Waggoner. The three girls left in the family
to eventually (God willing) get married.
And to all the girls who desire to honor and please God
through the gift of marriage, as well as the amazing moms
who raised them . . . this book was written for you.

. . . .

"Many women do noble things, but you surpass them all."
Charm is deceptive, and beauty is fleeting;
but a woman who fears the Lord is to be praised.
PROVERBS 31:29-30

Contents

Index of Prayers

How to use this book

eddings are wonderful, beautiful, a celebration of a new life—and lots of work. Whether you are the bride or her mother, the months ahead will be busy! Inside this book, you'll find tips to help you plan the entire experience, from the falling in love to the happily ever after. And if you start to get overwhelmed, the prayers in this book will clear your head and reset your focus.

Pray through the book together as you encounter the joy-filled moments and the stomach-dropping issues of planning for the big day. The first section includes prayers, Bible verses, tips, and challenges for the bride. The second section offers the same for the mother of the bride. If you live together, keep the book somewhere where you both can use it as you pray for the wedding, the groom, and each other. If you aren't living together, maybe trading the book back and forth once a week will work. Or buy one book for each of you if your wedding planning is done miles apart.

The two sections mirror each other so you will both be praying about the same topics at the same time. There are prayers for all aspects of marriage, character, planning, and the wedding itself. However, if you come across a prayer subject that doesn't pertain to you or your family, just skip it and move on. The idea is to cover your engagement period and wedding with as much prayer as possible and to learn to love and appreciate God as you are learning to love and appreciate each other.

The
Bride

Introduction

Congratulations!

You're getting married!

Wait . . . pause . . . let it sink in . . . *YOU. ARE. GETTING. MARRIED!*

As I write this, I am preparing for my wedding. In 352 days, I will say "I do!" to my fiancé, Parker—the man I love with all my heart; the man of my dreams; the one I have prayed for since I was a little girl; the man God created to be my husband. I have imagined what this would be like, and God has far exceeded my hopes and expectations. Every day I get more excited for the love and life that He has prepared for us. It's hard to believe that by the time you read this book, I'll be married—a Mrs.! It happens all the time, but when it happens to you, it's amazing and incredible and once-in-a-lifetime crazy. Hold on, the tears are flowing again—that's been happening a lot lately.

If you're anything like me, you probably have a serious case of "bride brain" right now. Wedding planning and all things bride-to-be are pretty much what you think about—period. The first few weeks after Parker proposed, I was overwhelmed with excitement. Immediately, I started searching the Internet and social media for wedding ideas and tips. I also went to our local bookstore and purchased the best wedding planning guidebook I could find. Please tell me you did the same.

As I write this, I'm finishing my last semester of college, and I often catch myself in class, daydreaming about wedding dresses, the ceremony, our first dance as a married couple, venue decorations, and everything else wedding related. It was hard to even sleep those first few weeks. In fact, I'm two months into our engagement and wedding preparations, and I'm finally starting to sleep at night, but the daydreaming continues.

Your wedding is a once-in-a-lifetime gift from God. It is by far one of the most important and exciting (and sometimes a bit stressful) times in your life! So go ahead and rock that bride brain because, before you know it, the big day will be here.

We still have months to go and tons of planning left to do, but here's where we are so far:

- We picked our wedding date: January 13, 2018.
- Over the last three decades, my mom and dad have developed a lot of important relationships and friendships; therefore, we have a substantial guest list. Finding a wedding/reception venue has been a huge challenge. I'd had my hopes set on a rustic country wedding, but most barns cannot hold the number of people we have on our invite list. You learn early on that compromise is vital when it comes to wedding planning. We've decided where the ceremony will be, but we're still searching for the reception venue.
- We've ordered our *Save the Date* cards.
- My maid of honor is none other than my incredible younger sister, Camryn! She's not only my sister and maid of honor, but my best friend. (Love you, Cam!)

And by the way . . . you're getting married!
Has it sunk in yet? Do you keep replaying those words in your mind?

While you plan and prepare for your wedding, God is preparing you to be a wife to the man of your dreams, the man He created just for you. God is giving you the desires of your heart; your prayers are being answered—He is always faithful and good!

Of course, I'm getting reminders from my mom too. "Oh my, it just hit me again . . . you are getting married!" She's not only the mother of the bride but she's the most important woman in my life. I pray that one day I'm a wife and mother like she is. We're constantly talking about wedding ideas, sending each other pictures of wedding shoes and dresses, coming up with ideas for bridesmaids' gifts, crying together, and laughing at how crazy it is that we're actually planning my wedding. But mostly, we pray. In fact, prayer is the reason you're holding this book in your hands. Prayer has been my lifeline—and it can be yours too!

Yes, you have to plan and do all the amazing things that go along with preparing for a wedding—pick a date, book a venue, create your guest list, send out invitations, choose your bridesmaids, taste test your wedding cake, find a dress, and so much more.

But all of this is secondary to prayer.

Prayer will not only prepare you for your wedding day, it should be the foundation upon which you build a lifetime with your husband. I've been praying for my future husband since I was ten years old. And as I pray for him, I find myself asking God to not only prepare Parker, but to prepare me as well. I know that oftentimes we focus on praying for everything and everyone else. But now is the time to seek the Lord on your own behalf—praying that He will prepare *you* for your husband.

This book is a lot of things, but mainly and most importantly, it's your personal, bride-to-be prayer guide. We've followed each prayer topic with relevant passages of Scripture that my mom and I have found to be essential and meaningful. After you read the verses, take time to meditate on what God's Word says and how you can apply these amazing truths to your life and marriage.

You'll also find some fun wedding tips that my wedding family (aka the incredible people who are walking alongside me through all of this) and I have learned along the way. I hope these tips not only encourage you and give you ideas, but make you laugh and enjoy every moment of being the bride-to-be.

Bride brain and all, God's got this—and He has immeasurably more than you could ever ask for or imagine planned for you. Are you with me? Let's pray . . .

LOVE THE LORD
AND EACH OTHER

Dear Lord,

Thank You for the gift of love. We cannot know what love is without You. You are the very definition of love; perfect, holy, unconditional love. The depth and breadth of Your amazing love is limitless. Everything that You are and do is wrapped up in love. Thank You for sending Your one and only Son, Jesus, to display Your love among us. Because of Him, we can love You and love others.

Jesus, You laid down Your life for us so that we can experience Your love and do the same. As husband and wife, please help us to lay down our lives for each other. Help our love, affection, and intimacy grow and strengthen one day at a time, for as long as we live. Please teach _____ to love me the way You love the church—completely, expectantly, unconditionally. It's hard to fathom this kind of love, but in Christ and through the power and presence of the Holy Spirit, I know it's possible. Father, help us never forget that marriage involves great sacrifice. Remind us that, just as Your sacrifice was worth it, the sacrifices You call us to make are always worth the price.

Thank You for loving me so perfectly that I can know, experience, and extend real, agape love. Let my love for _____ be a reflection of how much You love him. Please teach me to express my love, not only through words but also through actions and daily decisions. I want my fiancé to know more of Your infinite, unfailing love because, through Christ, I love him the way You love us.

Lord, I pray that when he needs it most, You would remind him how much You love him—and that some of these reminders would come through the way I love him. I believe that the more we grow in our relationship with You, the greater our love for You and each other will be. Father, please help

_____ to know You more, and as a result, love You more. Jesus, because of Your love, I pray that he would love me unconditionally and wholeheartedly. Help him to love the way You do, especially when it's hard. Lord, I pray that he would learn more each day how to express his love for me.

Heavenly Father, help us never lose sight of the depth and breadth of Your love. We need only look to the cross and the sacrifice Jesus made to remember the extent of Your love for all humankind. May our love for You and for each other grow daily as You continue to shape us into the image of Christ. You are and must always be our first love. Lord, help us to love You more than we love each other.

As 1 Corinthians 13:4–8 describes, I pray that our love for each other would be patient and kind, not self-seeking, boastful, envious, or easily angered. "Love does not delight in evil but rejoices with the truth" (1 Corinthians 13:6). Yes, Lord, keep us from evil and help us to speak the truth in love. God, just as You have forgiven us, please help us to extend forgiveness through love, never keeping record of the wrongs we have done. I pray that, like Your love, our love will always protect, trust, hope, persevere, and never fail.

Ultimately, I pray that our relationship will be an expression and reflection of Your love.

And through our love, let others experience Your love.

In Jesus's name, amen.

. . . .

For God so loved the world that he gave his one and only Son,
that whoever believes in him shall not perish but have eternal life.

JOHN 3:16

Dear Lord,

By the breath of Your mouth, You created us and filled our existence with great purpose. Apart from You, our lives have no meaning or purpose—we're just a heartbeat wrapped in flesh, waiting to draw the next breath. Without You we have nothing . . . We are nothing. Thank You for giving us everything we need for life and godliness through Your Son, Jesus. He fills our lives with earthly purpose and eternal significance.

Lord, thank You for creating _____ in Your image. Thank You for saving him and grooming him into everything You long for him to be. Father, please help him to never forget that he was made for more; that he was made for You. Earthly success and achievements are different from eternal treasures and rewards, and the pursuit of them produces very different men. Help _____ to seek the eternal over the temporary. Lord, if my fiancé's understanding of Your purpose for his life is unclear, please reveal that to him. Because ultimately, his purpose, my purpose, and our purpose as a married couple is to love You, to love others, and to share the truth of the gospel with the world. What a privilege!

Heavenly Father, I pray that _____ would see the greater purpose for his life unfold through what You've created him to do and be. May he never doubt Your grand design and the specific gifts You have given him to serve You and others. Please give him the confidence and courage to fulfill Your will for his life. Whatever he does, help him to do it for You and Your glory! Protect him from wasting the gifts and talents You have blessed him with. If there are gifts he is unaware of, please reveal them to him that he might bring You glory through them. Help me to encourage my future husband and see him the way You see him, Lord. Reveal to me the gifts You have given him and help me to champion him in those areas of his life.

Lord, I pray that wherever You lead us, we would hear Your voice and follow. Whenever we get discouraged, remind us that Your plans for our life together cannot be thwarted. Help us to know that we are never alone. You walk with us, one step and one breath at a time as we accomplish Your will. Lord, help me to respect, support, and trust my future spouse; help me believe that You have a perfect plan for our lives. Where You lead us, we will follow.

Not only is there divine purpose in our individual lives, but in our marriage as well. Please teach us the greater purpose for our marriage. It's not about us; it's about You. Marriage is about glorifying You and making You and Your great love known. Lord, I pray that when people see us, they get a glimpse of Jesus and the way He loves the church. Marriage is one of the greatest displays of Your love, so help us to honor and respect that in every way. Let us not waver from Your plan for our lives together.

Lord, guard our marriage as You daily motivate us to pursue righteousness and holiness. Please keep our hearts and minds fixed on You, so that we can live out our purpose both as individuals and as one.

In Jesus's name, amen.

. . . .

Jesus answered, "I am the way and the truth and the life.
No one comes to the Father except through me."

JOHN 14:6

A PRAYERFUL LIFE

Lord,

Prayer is amazing! The ability to come and talk to You with my heart wide open, just as I am—it's a treasure beyond measure. Thank You for hearing me and always knowing exactly what I need. Thank You for listening to me and for working everything in my life together for good.

Prayer is a vital part of my life. Preparing my heart through prayer to become a wife gives me confidence that You will walk alongside me through this incredible season. Sometimes I feel overwhelmed because there is so much to pray about. When I feel this way, please remind me that You are sovereign and good. That every day, You are at work preparing me to become one with my husband through the covenant of marriage. Lord, help me to not be anxious; instead, help me to pray about everything and trust You completely.

Lord, our marriage will not survive without prayer. Teach us how to pray and seek You together. Help us passionately pursue Your presence. God, during hard times, please help us not to just pray for our circumstances to change, but to seek to be changed by You in the midst of our circumstances. Lord, shape our prayer life so that we don't just come to You in times of need, but also to thank You, to spend time with You, and to enjoy Your presence.

Father, I am so thankful that You're always listening. Please help us pray according to Your will and believe that an answer is coming in Your perfect timing. When we don't receive the answer we were hoping and praying for, help us to praise You anyway. Lord, Your ways are not our ways; Your thoughts are not our thoughts. Please teach us to trust You, even when we don't understand Your decisions.

Heavenly Father, please help me and _____ to pray consistently together as a married couple. I don't want a single day to go by that we aren't seeking You as one. Lord, give us wisdom and teach us how to pray for each other. Convict our hearts; make us aware of anything in our lives that might hinder our prayers. My heart's desire, Lord, is that my prayers are even more fervent when it comes to praying for my husband. Show me how to come boldly to the throne of grace on his behalf. Give me supernatural insight, so I can pray for him according to Your will about matters that he might not even be aware of. Remind us when we pray that nothing is too hard for You!

Thank You for the gift of prayer. Help me never to lose sight of the tremendous blessing and responsibility it is to pray for my husband.

In Jesus's name, amen.

. . . .

When you call on me, when you come and pray to me, I'll listen.
When you come looking for me, you'll find me. Yes, when you get serious
about finding me and want it more than anything else,
I'll make sure you won't be disappointed.
JEREMIAH 29:12-14 MSG

Do not be anxious about anything, but in every situation,
by prayer and petition, with thanksgiving, present your requests to God.
And the peace of God, which transcends all understanding,
will guard your hearts and your minds in Christ Jesus.
PHILIPPIANS 4:6-7

TRUTH AND
THE WORD OF GOD

Dear Lord,

Thank You for Your Word, the truth that sets us free (John 8:31–32). If we know You and hold fast to Your truth, we can walk in freedom. Thank You, Lord, that in a world filled with lies, You are the truth and have provided a manual for life and godliness, Your Word, the Bible. Your Word is alive; it is living and at work in the lives of all who follow You.

God, I pray that You would renew _____'s mind with the truth of who You are and who he is in You. I pray that he would know the truth and that the truth would set him free to live for You wholeheartedly. Please continue to reveal Yourself to him as he seeks You daily through Your Word. Father, please hide Scripture in his heart so he can know You more, and so that he knows who he is in Christ. Your Word declares that this man, whom I love, is chosen and set apart, a child of the King of kings and Lord of lords. When he forgets, please remind _____ who You created him to be.

Lord, I pray that Your Word alone would be the anchor and foundation for our individual lives and our marriage. May we always use the sword of the Spirit to guard against the fiery arrows of the enemy.

The enemy has no power over the truth. You are truth. You are life. Darkness and evil cannot stand against the words You have spoken. Lord, I pray that Your words would be so deeply hidden in our hearts that we would immediately respond to temptation and fear with the power of Scripture.

Heavenly Father, please help us to believe every word You have spoken. Help us to not only believe what You've said, but to act on it and obey. Help us to speak the truth in love. I pray that the words we speak to one another will be filtered through a heart that is hidden in who You are.

Your Word endures forever; it will never fail. Your Word is a guiding lamp for our feet and a light for our path (Psalm 119:105). I pray that _____ and I would allow Your truth to always light our way. Help us to love and obey You, to live according to the words You have spoken.

Heavenly Father, thank You for sending Your Son so that Your Word became flesh (John 1:14). You are the Word, and in You we have everything we need. You are our lifeline! Please, Father, I pray that we would never lose sight of *who* the Word of God is. Remind us that these are not just words written and inspired by You, but that *You are* the Word!

This is the cry of my heart for the two of us:

His word is in my heart like a fire, a fire shut up in my bones. I am weary of holding it in; indeed, I cannot.

JEREMIAH 20:9

In Jesus's name, amen.

. . . .

The Word became flesh and made his dwelling among us.
We have seen his glory, the glory of the one and only Son,
who came from the Father, full of grace and truth.

JOHN 1:14

Jesus Calling by Sarah Young is one of my all-time-favorite devotionals. In fact, Parker and I have the *Jesus Calling* app on our phones so we can access it at any time. Every morning after we read that day's message, we talk about what we learned. Usually our devotion discussions lead to even deeper God talks—which I love. If you're not familiar with *Jesus Calling*, the author writes messages to the reader as if from God's point of view. So, in that spirit, for Bride Challenge #1, you're going to write your fiancé a letter from God's perspective. Tell him what you think God would say to him right now as he prepares to be your husband. Try to imagine what would be on God's heart and what you think He might share with him as he plans to enter into the covenant of marriage.

Before you start writing, pray. Ask God to reveal His desires for your future husband so you can share His words and His heart. When you're done writing the letter, place it in an envelope and pray again. Pray that when your fiancé reads the letter, he will be blessed and encouraged, and then move deeper into the love of God and your love for him. Oh, and think of a special time to either send it to him or give it to him in person.

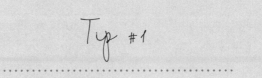

Tip #1

This is the day the Lord has made, let us *rejoice* and be glad in it!

Every day is a gift. Especially your wedding day! And trust me, everyone will tell you this, but it really does go by faster than you think. So stop and appreciate every single moment—and that includes every moment leading up to *the moment*.

Bride-to-be, I know it can be overwhelming. And I'm sure you've said more than once, "Can it just be my wedding day already?" Trust me, I get it. My first meltdown happened during our second week of planning. However, one of the most important things I learned during the wedding planning journey was to be thankful for every single moment—even the stressed out, want-to-cry-all-day, ditch-all-the-planning-and-elope moments. Let's be honest, if you don't cry at least once while you're planning your wedding, are you sure you are actually getting married, and are you human? But no matter how stressful it is, the planning isn't worth losing your mind over.

This is my first and most important tip: give thanks. First Thessalonians 5:18 says, "Give thanks in all circumstances; for this is God's will for you in Christ Jesus." *All circumstances* includes when your wedding dress doesn't turn out the way you hoped it would and you have to order new material to be shipped from across the world in order to make your dress into what you dreamed it would be. (Yes . . . this happened.) *All circumstances* means thanking God when you're experiencing serious bride brain and can't focus on anything for more than ten seconds before shifting your attention back to song selections and seating charts. *All circumstances* means *all* circumstances. Oftentimes during our many months of planning and meetings, I purposefully stopped in the middle of everything and started whispering, "Thank You, Lord. Thank You, Lord." Because at the end of the day, without Him, marriage would not have any value or meaning. It wouldn't exist, because without Him, love does not exist. He is love.

During the wedding planning craziness, you might find yourself getting caught up in the mountain of details and everything else going on, especially if things aren't moving forward the way you hoped and planned. To keep your heart and mind focused on God, what He is doing, and the blessing and covenant of marriage, consider keeping a journal of moments throughout the journey. Write down exactly what you're thinking and feeling; record specifically what you are most thankful for. Trust me, you will forget the little "God things" that happened along the way. Write them down and thank God for them.

I learned a lot during the twelve months it took to plan my wedding. Many times, I was so worried and anxious about decisions that had to be made that I missed the chance to embrace and appreciate the moment I was in. But the truth is, all we have is this moment. All we have is today. Your wedding and everything that leads up to it is a once-in-a-lifetime event. You will never get this time back. So rejoice! Thank God for choosing this amazing man who loves you and plans to spend the rest of his life with you. Praise God that He is working all things together for your good—including your wedding day.

TRUST

Lord,

Trust—it's not always easy to give, and it's even harder to get back once it's been lost. Thank You, Lord, that You are always trustworthy. Even when I don't understand, even when everything around me is falling apart, even when You're silent and I can't seem to hear You or reach You, I can trust that You are holding me and every area of my life safely in the palm of Your hand.

Lord, help me to trust You completely with everything regarding my wedding day and my marriage. From the smallest details to what matters most to me and everything in between, help me to trust You. But more importantly, please help me to trust You with _____. He is Yours. And by Your amazing grace, You have entrusted him to me to love, honor, respect, and cherish all my days here on this earth. What a blessing! What a privilege! Heavenly Father, I do not take this responsibility lightly. I know that I cannot be the godly wife that he needs without You. Thank You, Lord, for providing everything I need to take care of my future husband and for trusting me with his heart.

I pray, Lord, that _____ and I would place our trust and expectations in You. We cannot fully trust each other if we don't first trust You *with* each other. When doubt creeps into our lives, help us to resist the enemy and turn to You. Guide us back to the truth. Thank You for always being fully and completely trustworthy. You never waver. You always stay the same. Your Word is steadfast and true. Lord, my heart's desire is that no matter what happens in our lives, we will choose to trust and love You with all our heart, soul, mind, and strength.

God, You are sovereign and good. The words You have spoken are true and trustworthy. You are exactly who You say You are. You can and will do exactly what You have promised to do. I can fully rely on Your character and Word. You are God.

Lord, I pray that I will be able to trust my husband completely. Even though we are imperfect, and fall short, I pray that I can trust every word that comes out of _____'s mouth and know that he will follow through on commitments and promises he has made—the greatest being our marriage.

Father, I pray that lying and deceit will have no place in our home. Please guard and protect us against it in Jesus's name. If trust is ever broken in our relationship, I pray that we will come to You immediately; that we will seek You first for forgiveness and restoration.

Lord, keep us from trusting in our own abilities and strengths more than in who You are and what You have done. Remind us that You are in control. Help us not to just say that we trust You, but to really live out that trust in tangible ways. Help me to trust You completely with my future husband. And just as Abraham laid Isaac on the altar, may I have nothing in my life that means more than You. And I pray that my soon-to-be husband would live in the same way. Lord, let nothing matter more to him than You.

Thank You, Lord, that You are and always will be trustworthy.

In Jesus's name, amen.

. . . .

Whoever can be trusted with very little
can also be trusted with much,
and whoever is dishonest with very little
will also be dishonest with much.

LUKE 16:10

Heavenly Father,

You are perfect and holy. No one is like You. Your glory and goodness reach far beyond our ability to grasp or comprehend. Lord, help me to never lose sight of Your greatness. Please keep me in continuous awe of You.

Lord, we are far from perfect. We fail You daily, but the love and grace You extend to us never changes, regardless of our failures. You love us, no matter what. Thank You, Jesus, for making it possible for us to come boldly to the Father. We don't have to get it right before we come to You. This is so encouraging! Thank You for the freedom and forgiveness we have in You. Thank You, Father, for sacrificing Your Son so that we can be forgiven. Our sins are forgiven, and we are righteous in Your sight. Thank You that we stand before You, holy and redeemed through Jesus. It's amazing!

Your Word says in 1 John 1:9, "If we confess our sins, he is faithful and just and will forgive us our sins and purify us from all unrighteousness." Convict me, Lord, when I have sinned against You or hurt those whom You love. Show me when I am being unloving or harboring unforgiveness. Help _____ to do the same—to respond to the Holy Spirit's conviction and seek forgiveness and restoration. Help me to be a tangible representation of Your faithfulness and forgiveness in my husband's life.

Lord, I pray that in our marriage, _____ and I would forgive each other the way You have forgiven us. Colossians 3:13 says, "Bear with each other and forgive one another if any of you has a grievance against someone. Forgive as the Lord forgave you." Teach us how to extend grace and forgiveness, even when it may not be deserved; give us that same gracious and loving attitude toward each other that You have toward us.

I pray that we would not only be quick to forgive, but also quick to seek forgiveness. Reveal to us when we are in the wrong; keep our pride and arrogance from getting in the way of a repentant heart. Help us to seek holiness and humility above being right. May we never hold a grudge or be quick to become angry. Help both of us to live in the spirit of forgiveness. Even before we apologize, I pray that we would have already forgiven each other in our hearts.

Lord, living with a heart of forgiveness is only possible in Christ. Thank You for forgiving me, so that I can extend that same forgiveness to _____.
Please continue to shape our hearts to be more like You—especially when it comes to forgiving one another.

In Jesus's name, amen.

. . . .

For You, Lord, are good, and ready to forgive,
and abundant in mercy to all those who call upon You.
PSALM 86:5 NKJV

Be kind and compassionate to one another,
forgiving each other,
just as in Christ God forgave you.
EPHESIANS 4:32

Lord,

I have so much to be thankful for. So many blessings You have graciously poured into my life. I'm getting married! And every day is one day closer to that amazing day. Thank You for blessing me with _____, the godly man I will soon get to call my husband. I believe that before time began, You chose him for me. Thank You. You set us apart as Your very own and, at just the right time, You brought us together. It's amazing! As we prepare for our wedding and life together, please fill our hearts with gratitude. Remind us of all that You have done to bring us to this moment in time.

Lord, help us to be thankful for the little things and to always show our gratitude for one another. I pray that we would never take one another for granted. As _____'s wife, show me how to bless him so that he knows how loved and appreciated he is.

Father, 1 Thessalonians 5:18 tells us to be thankful in everything, because that's Your will for us. Lord, if it's Your will that we be thankful in all circumstances, give us the courage to do so, because life is hard. We all experience pain and heartache, and oftentimes giving thanks is the last thing we want to do. But regardless of the struggles, You are still God, and You are still good. Being thankful is not about how we feel in any given situation; it's about choosing to love and obey You and Your will for our lives. So, Lord, regardless of how we feel or what's going on in our lives, please help both of us to be thankful, no matter what.

Father, I know that we can come to You freely and ask You for anything, but Lord, I pray that when we seek You, our prayers will always be motivated by an attitude of gratitude. We don't deserve Your love. We don't deserve Your favor. We don't deserve Your blessings. But You still lavish us with everything we need and more. Thank You, Lord! Keep us from thinking that we can do life without You and guard us from becoming ungrateful. Help us to always be mindful and thankful for Your generosity, grace, and tender mercies.

Thank You, Lord, for blessing us beyond comprehension.

In Jesus's name, amen.

· ·

Enter his gates with thanksgiving and his courts with praise;
give thanks to him and praise his name.

PSALM 100:4

Whatever you do, whether in word or deed,
do it all in the name of the Lord Jesus,
giving thanks to God the Father through him.

COLOSSIANS 3:17

Always giving thanks to God the Father for everything,
in the name of our Lord Jesus Christ.

EPHESIANS 5:20

Heavenly Father,

As my fiancé and I prepare for our wedding, please bless us with wisdom and understanding so that we can know You better. As every day draws us one day closer to the big day, please give us greater knowledge of the depths of Your love, goodness, and sovereignty. We have so many decisions to make, but You know exactly what we need. We cannot do this without You, so please, intervene and give us clarity. Father, I pray that everything leading up to our wedding—every meeting, every decision, every prayer—would be accomplished through the wisdom You freely give us.

Lord, what a blessing and privilege it is to pray for this man who will soon be my husband. I have so much to pray about, but more than anything, I pray that _____ would humbly seek You with all his heart, soul, mind, and strength. Life is hard and filled with challenges. The world is full of distractions and temptations trying to pull him away from Your purpose and plan. Lord, please give him the wisdom to ignore the voices of the world and fiercely pursue the call You've placed on his life.

Surround him with godly men who will encourage and teach him, keep him accountable, and strengthen his relationship with You. Give him opportunities to encourage others as well. Lord, I pray that my future husband would always think before he speaks and that his words would be filled with humility. Help _____ to be wise in the way he acts toward others and may his conversations always be full of grace (Colossians 4:5–6). Let others want to gain spiritual wisdom by watching the way he lives.

Please guard our hearts and minds. Guard us against temptations and thoughts that don't please You. When the temporary things of this world vie for our attention, draw us back to our eternal purpose. Please continue to give us wisdom and discernment for all of life's decisions. When the direction is unclear, give us the patience and guidance we need to make the best godly choice. Lord, help _____ and me choose You and Your will above all else. I pray that we would consistently honor and glorify You in all we do and as a result, honor our marriage.

Lord, I pray that as a married couple, we would pursue wisdom and encourage each other in our walk with You. Let the wisdom You give us be manifest in every area of our lives. Father, because we are Yours, we have the mind of Christ. Help us to not only think like You but live like You, so that our actions reflect who You are. As we live to serve You one day at a time, please help us glorify and honor You.

In Jesus's name, amen.

· ·

The fear of the LORD is the beginning of knowledge,
but fools despise wisdom and instruction.
PROVERBS 1:7

For since in the wisdom of God the world through its wisdom
did not know him, God was pleased through the foolishness
of what was preached to save those who believe.
1 CORINTHIANS 1:21

Dear God,

Thank You for the gift of words and communication. Before a word comes out of my mouth, You already know what I am going to say. This gives me great confidence because I know that no matter what, You already know what I need and You always hear me.

Communication is vital in all relationships, but especially between a husband and wife. Thank You for giving _____ and me the ability to communicate. Help us to share what's on our hearts and minds so we can communicate effectively and grow in our knowledge and love for one another. I pray that we would put time and energy into learning and understanding each other; that we would communicate often so we can better appreciate each other's unique personalities, passions, and calling. Your Word says that You give us the Spirit of wisdom and revelation so that we may know You better. Lord, I pray that Your Spirit would not only help us to know You better, but to also understand and know each other better.

Lord, let our words be encouraging, loving, true, and sincere. I pray that we would always be authentic and upfront with one another. Break down any walls that would hinder us from experiencing open and honest communication in our marriage. Help us speak the truth in love. Let the words we speak be a reflection of who we are in Christ. Luke 6:45 tells us, "A good man brings good things out of the good stored up in his heart, and an evil man brings evil things out of the evil stored up in his heart. For the mouth speaks what the heart is full of." So I ask, God, may our hearts be filled with good!

Lord, I pray that You would give _____ the ability to speak with confidence and clarity. I pray that his words would continually encourage and build others up. Let the way he communicates be a reflection of Your heart and love for others. Help him to be a man of his word. If he says he's going to do something, I pray that he will follow through every time. Help him be slow to speak and react; make him patient and humble; let Your words come forth from his heart. I pray that every word from his mouth would be uttered with confidence but not arrogance.

Heavenly Father, I pray that people would desire to hear what _____ has to say because his words are filled with truth and life. May his peers look to him for wisdom and encouragement, respecting his integrity, faith, and insight.

Lord, please bless the way we communicate with each other and others. Help us speak words of life and to listen more than we speak. A vital part of communication is listening, so please give us ears to hear each other and fully understand what is being spoken. When words are not needed, help us be silent. When words are needed, help us speak the truth with grace and kindness. Father, help us to know when to be silent, when to listen, and when to speak.

In Jesus's name, amen.

. . . .

A gentle answer turns away wrath, but a harsh word stirs up anger.
PROVERBS 15:1

Don't shoot off your mouth, or speak before you think.
Don't be too quick to tell God what you think he wants to hear.
God's in charge, not you—the less you speak, the better.
ECCLESIASTES 5:2 MSG

irlfriend, are you ready for this? It's very important. I hope you loved your first challenge because this one is going to be similar. However, instead of writing to your fiancé, you are going to write a thank-you letter to your parents (or whomever you feel has had the greatest impact on your life). Tell them how grateful you are for their influence and investment in your life. Be as specific as possible as you explain all they have meant to you and why. Again, pray before you start writing and ask God to help you share your heart.

Okay, I was just thinking, maybe you're juggling a hectic, busy, bride-to-be schedule right now. I get it. If you don't have time to write a letter, at the very least, send your parents a card. They've loved and raised you, provided for you in multiple ways, and made sacrifices for your well-being that you will never know about. Now would be a good time to let your parents know how much you appreciate them and all they have done for you.

Tip #2

*B*efore we dig into this tip, you and I need to come to an understanding about a few things. You are beautiful. Not because I said so, not because your husband-to-be has told you so hundreds of times, and not because when you look in the mirror, your outward appearance reflects what the world defines as beautiful. No; you're beautiful because God purposefully and wonderfully designed and knit you together. He created you and knew everything about you before you were born. No one else besides your Creator can define your beauty.

Your beauty comes from within. People look at your outward appearance, but the Lord looks at your heart. When your heart is in a right relationship with God, He allows your outward appearance to radiate in a way that the best makeup or hairstyle cannot touch. In fact, the radiance I'm talking about sets you apart in ways nothing else can.

A few days after I got engaged, I made a list of beauty tips I wanted to address in preparation for my wedding. A bride wants to look her absolute best on her wedding day. From hair and makeup to the bridal shower; from the rehearsal outfit to the wedding dress—we want everything to be perfect. And there's nothing wrong with this—unless it becomes an obsession that distracts you from preparing your heart to be a godly wife.

I get it! I've been distracted and obsessed, and it's unhealthy on so many levels. But I've also prayed and learned a lot. As a result, my perspective has changed regarding all the wedding day beauty preparations. Yes, I still want to be beautiful on my wedding day. But it's for the glory of God first and foremost and then, of course, my husband. Ultimately, these beauty tips are about presenting your best outward appearance, so that you can show the greater beauty of what's inside.

Take Esther, for example. Esther 2:12 says, "Before a young woman's turn came to go in to King Xerxes, she had to complete twelve months of beauty treatments prescribed for the women, six months with oil of myrrh and six with perfumes and cosmetics." I'm not too sure about getting drenched in the oil of myrrh, but from what the Bible says, Esther literally prepared her outward appearance for a year before she went to meet the king. Also, how cool is it that they had beauty treatments back then! Instead of Estée Lauder, maybe it was called Esther Lauder. Just sayin'!

What I want to say here is, when you're preparing your outward self, don't forget to prepare your heart and mind too. Ask God to shape your heart to love like He loves and to prepare you daily to be a godly wife who radiates beauty from the inside out.

I'm sure you have your own beauty essentials that are different from mine, but I thought I would share mine with you anyway. Here's what I wrote down in my journal:

BEAUTY TIPS

- *Olaplex* (at least two times a week). For those who don't know what this is, it's a hair product that keeps your hair soft, healthy, and nourished.

- *Teeth Whitening.* You might be blessed with super white, sparkling teeth. If not, getting those teeth ready for wedding pictures and more than forty-eight hours of smiling and talking to guests is an absolute must and worth the investment. Crest brand is great, but believe it or not, Target's teeth whitening strips are even better, and they're cheaper too.

- *Biotin and keratin* (every day). These are in the vitamin family, but it's always best to check with your doctor before taking any supplement. Vitamin B7 (biotin) is also good for hair, skin, and nails.

- *Facials.* Although I'm sure you wash your face daily, getting a facial a few times before your wedding is a great idea. Your skin is your largest organ, and due to the numerous outside elements and toxins, it takes a daily beating. Getting a few facials leading up to your wedding day can help revitalize and cleanse your skin in ways that simple washing cannot. Some over-the-counter facial masks and peels are great and provide a more affordable option.

- *Work out.* I will share more about this in Tip #3, when I talk about "shredding for the wedding," but honestly, my main fitness goal has been and continues to be to firm up the booty. (I hope you're laughing.) Maybe you're blessed in this area (literally, LOL). God bless you! I'm thankful for what the good Lord gave me, but it's a work in progress, if you know what I mean.

- *Eat healthy.* This is an obvious beauty tip. What you eat directly affects your body, mind, emotions, and overall well-being. It's time to make some sacrifices. Hopefully, in doing so, you'll find that eating healthier actually changes more than just your health and outward appearance.

Hey, if you have more beauty tips you'd like to share with future brides, feel free to connect with me through my Instagram page: @thebridecollection so we can share your ideas with our followers. I'm excited to hear what you have to say.

CALLING

Lord,

You have called us to be Your children. Your disciples. Your hands and feet upon the earth. Your light in the midst of darkness. You have called us to love others and treat them the way You would. To live our lives worthy of the gospel. To speak the truth in love about who You are and what You have done. Lord, we are called to holiness and obedience, to love You above all else.

Heavenly Father, sometimes we forget what our true calling is because we get so caught up in trying to figure out what our "earthly calling" is. Lord, I pray that _____ and I would never lose sight of our heavenly calling. When we become one on our wedding day, I ask You to set a fire deep down in our hearts to pursue Your calling for our lives. We will no longer be two, but one; and we will pursue where You lead us *together*.

Father, I pray that my soon-to-be husband would be diligent and dedicated in following You. I pray that Your calling on his life would take root in his heart and mind and become the reason for his existence. Lord, as a married couple, help us fulfill the greatest calling—to love You and make You known. Let us never forget that where You call one of us, You call both of us. Because You are joining us together to follow where You lead, please keep us from making decisions on our own. Guide and protect us, Lord. Help us to seek You together before every decision we make in our lives. Give us courage and confidence in You so that when we hear You say "go," we will go without reservation or hesitation.

God, I believe You created us with gifts and talents so that we can bless and serve You and Your kingdom. Whether we work as doctors, lawyers, professional athletes, pastors, authors, or stay-at-home parents . . . whatever we do, it is meant to bring You glory. So I pray that, no matter what You have called each of us to do on this earth, we will gratefully serve You and never lose sight of our true calling.

Heavenly Father, please give _____ confidence, courage, and conviction in what You have called him to do. When he gets discouraged or has doubts, remind him that You will strengthen him and carry him through. Please help him to trust You and follow You even when he cannot see the road ahead. Thank You for all that You will do in and through my future husband. May Your glory be evident in his life. And together, as husband and wife, I pray that we would passionately live out our *greater calling.*

Be magnified through us, Lord.

In Jesus's name, amen.

. . . .

He has saved us and called us to a holy life—
not because of anything we have done but because
of his own purpose and grace. This grace was given us
in Christ Jesus before the beginning of time.

2 TIMOTHY 1:9

To this you were called, because Christ suffered for you,
leaving you an example, that you should follow in his steps.

1 PETER 2:21

Dear Lord,

Our character reveals who we are, what is most important to us, and the way we interpret, understand, and live life. Our character is vital to living a life that honors You above all else.

Heavenly Father, You know the real, unedited, and authentic me. You know every part of who I am—the good, the bad, the ugly . . . everything. Despite the flaws I see when I look in the mirror, You see the redeemed, set-apart woman of God You created. Because of the work You started in my life, my character is being molded and shaped into the image of Christ every day. Thank You, Lord, that I can trust You to complete the good work You started in me.

Lord, help _____ to honor and glorify You through his life. Mold his character into the image of Christ. Help him to be honest and walk in humility, especially when no one is looking. Father, I pray that my fiancé would have a godly reputation and gain the respect of those You have placed in his life. Lord, please give him a servant's heart so he can recognize and try to meet the needs of others. As he prepares to be my husband, help him love, honor, and respect me in every way. Make me worthy of those things, Lord, and let him know how much I respect, love, and honor him as well.

I pray that _____ would walk in integrity. That everything he says and does would be a reflection of Christ. As You build his character, I pray that he would kneel before You in prayer so he can stand up for what is right, true, and praiseworthy. Help him to be upfront and honest and never allow anything to stay hidden or lurk in the darkness. I pray that his actions would be an expression of his relationship with You.

Lord, help _____ be a man of virtue and honor. That he would desire to be pure in heart, mind, and body. Please remind him where his strength comes from, so that he can be courageous and vigilant in life's battles. God, as my husband, I pray that he would pray for me and protect me.

Lord, I pray that _____ would be a leader who brings people to the truth by sharing it in word, but more importantly, by his example. As he honors You with his life, may he gain the honor and respect of others. Please help him be a godly leader in our marriage and for our children one day. Father, I pray that our children would look to You because of the way their earthly father leads and loves his family.

Lord, help both of us to live above reproach so that people see You through us. May our lives and especially our marriage be a direct reflection of who You are. Keep jealousy, arrogance, and pride far from our home and help us to respond to each other with gentleness and patience. Father, please help us to always love, respect, and honor each other as we live for You one day at a time.

In Jesus's name, amen.

. . . .

Turn my heart toward your statutes and not toward selfish gain.
Turn my eyes away from worthless things;
preserve my life according to your word.
PSALM 119:36–37

Honor one another above yourselves.
ROMANS 12:10

Lord,

Thank You for choosing _____ for me. I cannot wait to be his wife, to grow old with him. To share life's many ups and downs, dreams, and hardships. To bear one another's burdens and share one another's joys . . . to spend a lifetime together learning, loving, and maturing in our relationship with You and each other . . . through life's many trials and triumphs.

Lord, we have so much to learn and experience. When I ponder this in my heart, I get excited and a bit fearful. I don't know all there is to know about my fiancé, and he doesn't know all there is to know about me.

How will he feel and what will he do when we find out that I am pregnant with our first child or if we learn we can't have children? When he is disappointed, confused, or frustrated as he strives to lead me and our family—how will he respond? I have so many questions and so much to discover about my future husband. He is a gift I long to unwrap each day—his desires, his passions, his thoughts, fears, and the motivations of his heart. There are so many unknown dimensions, and I long to see and know every one.

Father, I pray that _____ would desire to know everything about me as well, including the hidden and sacred things only You know. The more we draw near to You, the more we draw near to each other. Our learning and growing depends on You. The deeper we press into Your heart, the deeper we'll also press into each other's. Being one with You literally makes us one with each other at the most intimate level.

Please bless both of us with teachable, willing spirits. Help us to passionately and daily pursue You and Your Word so that we learn and grow in our faith. We are a work in progress, growing in unique ways to become who You created us to be. Your Word says in Philippians 1:6 that You began a good work in us and have promised to complete it. Thank You for this promise, Lord. We trust that You are doing in us what we could never do in our own strength.

Help _____ and me grow in respect and love for each other. Teach us how to be kind, patient, and gracious as we learn more about each other. Help us to remember that our intimacy and covenant with You must take precedence over every other relationship. You must always come first. Father, help us to be willing, open, honest, and vulnerable. Please keep our relationship vibrant and alive. Protect us from complacency, spiritual disconnection, or boredom.

Lord, You know what is best for us. Please teach, counsel, and guide us one day at a time. Keep us attentive, alert, and receptive to Your guidance and help us to want to follow Your lead. Protect us from worldly desires that would tempt us to try to go our own way. Please help us to diligently seek You through Your Word in every area of our relationship and lives. Help us to trust You to show us the way. Lead us into the good works You planned in advance for us to walk into as individuals and as a married couple. Lord, as sheep are fully dependent on the shepherd's voice, please help us to be completely dependent upon, attentive to, and always aware of Your voice, so we can distinguish it from all the other voices vying for our attention and loyalty.

In Jesus's name I pray, amen.

. . . .

Teach me how to live to please you, because you're my God.
PSALM 143:10 MSG

Dear Lord,

You are the giver of all good things. Thank You for providing everything we need. Because of Your generosity, we are blessed beyond measure. Thank You, heavenly Father!

Lord, please help my fiancé and me to be good stewards of everything You have entrusted to us. Thank You for the ability You've given us to work and earn a living. Lord, help us to see everything that pertains to our finances in the light of Your kingdom and to remember that everything we have, including the money we earn, belongs to You!

Father, please help _____ not to worry about finances or fear that he won't be able to provide. Help him to trust You and believe that You are his provider. You know what we need. I pray that he would appreciate his job and work hard every single day for Your glory. Help him to lead our home spiritually and financially. Keep us from laziness; help us remember that whatever work we do, we do it for You.

When it comes to spending, help us to be wise and to seek You first in all our financial decisions, no matter how big or small. Please help us to be mindful and strategic in our spending for the wedding. It can be expensive! Of course, we want everything to be amazing, but we don't have to spend a fortune to make that happen. Please give us discernment so we can know what to spend money on and what not to. Lord, thank You for providing everything we need for our wedding and reception.

Father, I pray that as a couple, we will always respect one another and seek each other's opinion on finances and spending before making decisions. Keep this from becoming an area of strife in our marriage. Lord, let money never become an idol in our home. Show us how to use the money we have in a way that glorifies and honors You. Help us be faithful in what You have called us to do with every penny.

Lord, what a tremendous blessing it is to be able to give. Help us to be generous. I pray that we would never give reluctantly but cheerfully, appreciating every opportunity we have to give back. Teach us how to give and show us where to give. Grant us generous lives for Your glory. Lord, I pray that You would bless us with the ability to give abundantly. Thank You that giving is a gift and a blessing, so please keep us from greed, hoarding, and a covetous spirit.

Father, whether we are in a season of abundance or great need, help us to be thankful, satisfied, and content with what we have. No matter how much we have, please help us never waver from giving freely. Please help us to store up treasures in heaven and not on this earth. And please, God, remind us that our greatest treasure is You—the Giver and not the gift.

In Jesus's name, amen.

. . . .

For where your treasure is, there your heart will be also.
MATTHEW 6:21

Give to everyone who asks you, and if anyone takes
what belongs to you, do not demand it back.
LUKE 6:30

Heavenly Father,

What a gift it is to laugh!

As _____ and I prepare to get married and spend the rest of our lives together, bless us with a healthy sense of humor that leads to lasting joy. Fill our hearts with gratitude and our home with laughter. When the cares of this world leave us broken and heavy-hearted, please break through the darkness with Your immeasurable joy. Father, please bless us with time spent laughing with family and friends, the kind of belly laugh that makes our stomachs ache and tears roll down our cheeks.

Lord, Your Word says there is a time for everything, including a time to cry and a time to laugh (Ecclesiastes 3:2–4). And even sometimes laughing so hard that you cry! I praise You for both seasons, for moments in life that my future husband and I will weather and enjoy together. Father, when brokenness and difficulty come, thank You that our tears won't last forever. At just the right time, You will replace our tears with rejoicing and laughter as Psalm 30:5 assures us, "For his anger lasts only a moment, but his favor lasts a lifetime; weeping may stay for the night, but rejoicing comes in the morning."

Heavenly Father, thank You for preparing me to become _____'s wife. As his wife, please help me to bring him joy and laughter like no one else can. Lord, even amid our busy lives, I pray that he would look forward to spending time with me and that being together would bless us both because of how much fun we have when we're together. When _____ is discouraged and hurting, I pray that the joy You give me would bring him peace and comfort. Please help me to know when he needs to laugh and when he needs me to cry with him.

Both tears and laughter are a gift from You. Help us to cherish and treasure both and not take them for granted. No matter how old we are or how long we've been married, please allow our sense of humor to grow and may our laughter and joy never end!

In Jesus's name, amen.

. . . .

A cheerful heart is good medicine,
but a crushed spirit dries up the bones.

PROVERBS 17:22

Our mouths were filled with laughter, our tongues with songs of joy.
Then it was said among the nations,
"The LORD has done great things for them."
The LORD has done great things for us, and we are filled with joy.

PSALM 126:2–3

There is a time for everything, and a season for every
activity under heaven . . . a time to weep and a time to laugh,
a time to mourn and a time to dance.

ECCLESIASTES 3:1, 4

Challenge #3

We all get the same twenty-four hours each day; no one gets a minute more or a minute less. Your mission for today is to set aside fifteen minutes. Do whatever you have to do to free up the time. If you're already thinking about how hard it's going to be to find these fifteen minutes, you're not alone. I'm right there with you. It seems like my life is running a hundred miles an hour right now, especially with the many responsibilities unique to wedding planning added to everything else I have going on. But, as you and I both know, we make time for what matters most to us.

Thus, your challenge, should you make the time to accept it, is simply this: *thank God*. Don't ask Him for anything, just spend fifteen minutes thanking Him for everything that comes to mind. It might be a good idea to have a pen and journal handy so you can write everything down. It's amazing how your perspective and heart can change when you purposefully take time out of a busy day to reflect on the many things you're grateful for and express that gratitude back to God.

This is the first time I have ever talked or written about my struggle. Although I'm feeling a bit apprehensive and vulnerable, I know that sharing will help not only me, but you as well.

I have struggled with my body image for a long time. Unfortunately, I wish I could say that I am no longer fighting the battle, but even now, God is doing a mighty, ongoing work in my heart, healing and conforming me into the image of His Son. To say that this has been a difficult road would be an understatement. If I could have picked a different struggle, I would have. However, by God's amazing grace, I am learning how to be content in every circumstance, whether my jeans fit or not.

Because I have dealt with body-image issues for what feels like forever, getting my body in the best possible shape for my wedding day and my future husband has been a balancing act. I wanted to put in the work and sacrifice, but I did not want to fall for the old tricks the way I used to—like looking in the mirror and never being satisfied; trying every supplement under the sun with little or no success; feeling defeated, worrying what other people think; obsessing over protein bars and powders; or condemning myself for enjoying an occasional sweet treat. It's *exhausting*. I cannot and will not go down that road again, so help me, God.

Instead, I chose to shred for the wed in a more God-glorifying way. I'm sure you've heard other brides toss this cliché around. It's a fun way of saying

"It's time to get my body prepared and ready for my husband." This may look different for you than it did for me. Maybe you're not trying to lose weight or pump up your physique. Either way, whatever "shredding for the wedding" looks like for you, it is important to do it in a way that glorifies God.

Rather than focusing on how and what I wanted my body to look like, I chose instead to fix my eyes on Christ and give my worries and insecurities to Him. I decided to be specific about every aspect of what I hoped to accomplish leading up to my wedding day. I decided I would trust Him with the outcome. He already knows the desires of my heart; He knows what motivates me. I can't pretend or hide from God, so why not put it all out there? As my mom often says, "Do your best and give God the rest."

So, what are some practical shredding-for-the-wedding tips? Glad you asked. We all have different body types and metabolism rates, so what works for me may not work for you. But there are things you can do that are a one-size-fits-all approach to fitness and body care.

Trust me, I'm not a health and fitness expert, but I've learned a lot in the six years I've spent working out and eating healthy. Here are a few things that I try to implement into my daily routine. They are overall health tips, so they'll benefit anyone.

10 WAYS TO GET SHREDDING
FOR THE WEDDING

1. *Get your sweat on!* Some people hate working out; just the thought of a treadmill makes them run in the opposite direction (but at least that's a small workout—just sayin'). But I'm one of those crazy types who *loves* working out. I'm a six-times-a-week, sweatin'-bullets kinda girl. Working out not only keeps me healthy and fit, it also relieves stress and anxiety. If you're just getting started in the fitness world, though, you don't need to jump in with such intensity. Start small.

Go for a walk or run. Do a workout video at home. Do whatever you need to do to get yourself moving.

2. *Eat healthy.* Easy to say; not always easy to do. My diet consists of lots of proteins, veggies, fruits, and healthy carbs. I've also chosen to cut out gluten for my own health purposes. Don't get me wrong, I eat ice cream and yummy (unhealthy) food sometimes, but I try to keep my daily routine as healthy as possible. Just think, whatever you put in your body should be fueling your temple so that you can serve God to the best of your ability.

3. *Drink water . . . lots and lots of water.* Staying hydrated is key, not just in your day-to-day life, but especially when working out and eating healthy. One of my favorite daily drinks is water with freshly squeezed lemon in it. *So* good! Cut out the sugary, fruity drinks—they just add calories and pour unhealthy ingredients into your body.

4. *Protein shakes for the win!* I love protein shakes and drink them daily as meal replacements or an after-workout replenish drink. All you need is a yummy protein powder (I prefer pea protein), unsweetened almond or coconut milk, banana, and cinnamon . . . and, of course, a blender. There are a ton of good protein shake mixes out there, and some sell samples so you can try them first to see if you like the taste.

5. *Eat.* Some people think that extensively cutting calories will get you skinny and keep you skinny. While cutting calories at first may help you lose weight, after a while, if you don't give your body enough nutrients, it will hurt your metabolism. Trust me, I've been there. Eating enough of the *right* foods is essential. My suggestion is to consult with a nutritionist to help point you in the right direction.

6. *Snack attack.* Prepare awesome healthy snacks ahead of time so you have them ready throughout the day. Rather than eating three big meals daily, I try to consistently eat smaller portions of good food

throughout the day. Having healthy snacks available—like veggies, fruits, and nuts—helps make my eating habits clean and easy.

7. *Rest!* At the very least, your body needs one full day to rest and recover each week. My day of rest is Sunday. I like to take a day off from all physical activity. I'm not only resting physically, but also emotionally and spiritually.

8. *Fix your eyes on Jesus, not on your body image.* This was a huge struggle for me. I became so consumed with how my body looked that I lost sight of the One who created my body in the first place. Whenever you feel overwhelmed or discouraged, remind yourself that your Creator knit you together and designed your body.

9. *Thank God for the body He's given you.* When you thank God consistently, no matter what your body looks like, more than just your attitude will change.

10. *Get your heart in shape before your body.* If your heart isn't in the right place, you can't expect your body to be. This is something I remind myself of daily, to focus on Jesus instead of my circumstances. Rather than obsessing about perfecting my body for my wedding day, I ask God to prepare my heart.

You want to look your best on your wedding day (and long after). Ultimately, shredding for the wedding should be about radiating the greater beauty of your heart through your outward appearance. Ask God to shape your heart to love like He loves and to prepare you daily to be a godly wife.

One day at a time. You've got this. But more importantly, He's got you!

Lord,

You are all we need and all we could ever want. And yet, too often we look in all the wrong places to fill our deepest need. Forgive us, heavenly Father.

I pray that You would be our greatest desire and first priority. No matter what our lives look like, help us to put You above everything else. Keep us from placing anything before You, especially each other. Help us to daily encourage each other in our pursuit of You. And as we become one, please be the greatest desire in our marriage.

Lord, as _____ and I prepare for our wedding day, remind us of what's most important. Keep our priorities steadfast on what matters most. The flowers, the cake, the music, the guests . . . they're all important. However, nothing compares to the core meaning of why we are getting married. Help us to never forget the magnitude and holiness of this covenant. Remind us that marriage is meant to last a lifetime and that when we say "I do," we become each other's greatest priority outside of our relationship with You. If You are our first priority, we will prioritize each other.

Teach me how to love my fiancé like You do and help me to keep him a top priority in my life. Keep me from ever putting my own needs above his, and please teach him to do the same. Together, let us pursue You first and, in turn, grow in our pursuit of one another. We will have seasons when life feels crazy and out of control, but I pray that, especially in those times, we would make each other a priority. I pray that nothing in this world would keep us from daily serving and loving one another. Lord, I pray that _____ and I would date each other for the rest of our lives, that our love would only grow and deepen with time.

Lord, one day if/when we have a family, be our priority above all else. I pray that any children we may have would grow up knowing that You come first, before everything and anyone. I pray that You would be all that matters to them as well. Mold and shape both of us now so that if we are blessed to be parents, our children see that You are the most important thing in our lives.

When we begin to chase after worldly desires or put anything before You, Lord, realign our priorities. Refocus our hearts so they are in tune with You and what You have planned and prepared for us. Your Word says that where our treasure is, there our heart will be also (Luke 12:34). Lord, may our greatest and most sacred treasure always be You. Thank You for being all that we need. Let us never forget who You are and what You have done.

In Jesus's name, amen.

. . . .

Very early in the morning, while it was still dark, Jesus got up, left the house, and went off to a solitary place, where he prayed.
MARK 1:35

But seek first his kingdom and his righteousness, and all these things will be given to you as well.
MATTHEW 6:33

For where your treasure is, there your heart will be also.
LUKE 12:34

Dear Lord,

Thank You for the gift of marriage. Marriage is a lifelong commitment to unconditional love, sacrifice, and selflessness. It's a commitment that is utterly impossible without You. You created marriage, and You are the only One who can sustain and protect it. Your character and the fruit of the Spirit are foundational to the covenant of marriage. Lord, I pray that as I anticipate and ready myself to meet my future husband at the altar, You would prepare me to die to myself and wholeheartedly live for You. Thank You, Jesus, for the sacrifice You made for me through dying on the cross, so that by the power of Your spirit, I can die to myself, take up my cross, and follow You.

Lord, I pray that _____ and I would enter our marriage aware and prepared to live sacrificially and selflessly. This is a one-day-at-a-time, one-prayer-at-a-time surrender. I am not perfect, and neither is _____. We need Your forgiveness, grace, and mercy on a daily basis in order to live the life You have called us to through our marriage. Please help us, Lord. Bless us with wisdom and knowledge so that we can understand and know what changes we need to make to better serve You and each other. Thank You for the privilege it is to serve him and love him sacrificially, to put his needs before my own. Lord, I pray that loving this man the way You do would be a focal point in my prayer life. Let my heart beat to bless him in any and every way that I can.

Thank You, Lord, for my fiancé and his desire to know and follow You. I pray that he would cling to You all the days of his life. Heavenly Father, I pray that his love for You would grow daily and that he would love You more than anything else in this world. May he be a man of sacrifice and selflessness who always puts others before himself. But more than anything, I pray that _____ would be a man after Your heart. That he would set aside all worldly pursuits and gains, in order to put You first. That the way of the cross would be an everyday reality, not merely a spiritual exercise.

Lord, prepare _____'s heart for our marriage and life together. Help him to live a life of humility and selflessness. I pray that You would remove any trace of pride or arrogance from him. May the sacrifices he chooses to make in our marriage be rewarded with more of You. Because our greatest sacrifices lead to our greatest gain—*You.*

Lord, may we always desire You more than anything else in this world. Help us to put You first, to die to ourselves daily as we serve You and each other. Help us surrender and confess our selfish desires to You so we can gain forgiveness. Motivate us to give all that we have for the sake of Your kingdom.

Help us to never lose sight of the ultimate sacrifice that Jesus made on our behalf so that we can passionately live for Him.

In Jesus's name, amen.

. . . .

Do nothing out of rivalry or conceit, but in humility consider others as more important than yourselves.
PHILIPPIANS 2:3 HCSB

No one should seek their own good, but the good of others.
1 CORINTHIANS 10:24

FREEDOM

Dear Lord,

In You, we are free! We are not bound. We are not stuck. The chains are gone. True and lasting freedom is found in You and You alone!

Lord, freedom is not free. You've graciously and willingly paid the ultimate price. You made the absolute sacrifice. You broke the chains we could never break. On the cross, You took upon Yourself the sin of the world so that we could be set free to love You and live for You. I am amazed and eternally grateful that You in all Your holiness, purity, and righteousness would willingly set free a sinner like me.

Jesus, I pray that _____ and I would never get over the sacrifice You made on our behalf. As we learn to recognize and appreciate what You have done and the power in Your sacrifice, help us walk in the freedom You bought for us. Please keep us from allowing the treasures of this world to fool us into thinking that they can satisfy. You alone are more than enough. Lord, help us to fully know that *we are free*—we don't have to continually ask You to set us free, because You took care of that on the cross! Thank You, Lord! You are amazing!

Lord, if _____ is approaching our wedding day weighed down by burdens or any sort of bondage, please make it known to him. If he has given power or authority to anything or anyone but You, show that to him. As he prepares for our wedding day, break any chains or bondage to sin that would keep him from the freedom You purchased for him.

Thank You, Lord, for the freedom that comes with being husband and wife. Marriage is such a beautiful picture of freedom. When _____ and I are married, we will be free in every aspect: spiritually, emotionally, physically, sexually, and more. There is purity and wholeness in being one, so help me,

Lord, to live freely with my husband. Allow my heart, mind, and body to be free in every way. And I pray the same for _____. I am his and he is mine.

Keep us from using our spiritual freedom to indulge in the flesh, but rather, help us to exemplify who You are to those around us (Galatians 5:13–14). When people see that we live freely in accordance with Your Word, I pray that they would long to know You. May the freedom we have in You be so evident in our lives that, when others are around us, they feel as though their own shackles are falling off. Only You can do this, Lord. Let them see Your mighty power at work within us.

Thank You for the extraordinary freedom You give through marriage. Help us to live our lives completely free!

In Jesus's name, amen!

. . . .

It is for freedom that Christ has set us free. Stand firm, then,
and do not let yourselves be burdened again by a yoke of slavery.
GALATIANS 5:1

To [those] who had believed him, Jesus said,
"If you hold to my teaching, you are really my disciples.
Then you will know the truth, and the truth will set you free."
JOHN 8:31–32

Heavenly Father,

Help us to remember that Christ is greater than our circumstances. Courage isn't easy. Stepping out in faith can be the hardest decision, because we don't know what lies ahead. But *You* know, and You go before us and promise to never leave us nor forsake us (Deuteronomy 31:8). Furthermore, You promise to be with us wherever we go (Joshua 1:9). Because You are strong and courageous, we have the power to be strong and courageous too. These truths are so comforting and encouraging.

I pray, Lord, that You would give _____ valiant courage and remind him that fear has no power—the enemy has already been defeated! Because of the cross, we are victorious!

In moments when he can't hear Your voice or when the path ahead seems long and daunting and he doesn't know where to go or what to do . . . please give _____ the courage to trust You and Your promises. Help him to rest in Your love, sovereignty, perfect will, and timing. It takes courage and strength to believe that everything is going to be okay even when it's not okay. It takes great faith to believe that You are Lord when our circumstances seem completely out of control. Please help _____ to trust that You are working all things together for good even when things do not appear to be good. Because You are always with him, please help him to have the courage to step out of his comfort zone into the realm of the unknown.

Lord, I pray that You would keep both of us from becoming comfortable or complacent. To be honest, it takes courage to pray this because I know courage sometimes comes through adversity and difficult experiences— by facing the giants in life. Still, I ask that You would lead us and fill us with great courage. Thank You that, in Christ, we already have everything we need to be brave. In the shadow of the unknown, remind us that You know, and that's enough. When the waves of life get rough and the storm begins to surround us, help us to rest in You.

I pray, Lord, that You would prepare _____ to face life's deepest, darkest valleys and help him to be strong and courageous—to fear no evil as he makes his way through life. Deepen his dependence on You now so that when trials come, he will cling to You, trusting that You have greater plans. Lord, I pray that we would encourage one another to be brave—to not conform to the pattern of this world, but to live for Christ and wholeheartedly follow Him.

Lord, marriage in and of itself demands courage; it means laying down our lives for each other and putting our spouse before ourselves. It means loving deeply without reservation and walking together through life, no matter how difficult it might get.

Marriage is a life of sacrifice. So Father, please prepare us every day to be sacrificial and courageous in our marriage and life together.

In Jesus's name, amen.

. . . .

Be strong and courageous. Do not be afraid or terrified because of them,
for the LORD your God goes with you; he will never leave you nor forsake you.
DEUTERONOMY 31:6

Be on your guard; stand firm in the faith; be courageous; be strong.
1 CORINTHIANS 16:13

Dear Lord,

Thank You for the comfort and compassion You freely give us. Thank You for being gracious, slow to anger, and abounding in love. Father, Your Word says that You are close to the brokenhearted and save those who are crushed in spirit. This is so comforting and encouraging. Thank You for taking care of us at all times, but especially during seasons of pain and heartbreak.

Lord, I pray that I offer the same comfort and compassion in my marriage. When _____ is in pain, fill me with empathy and understanding so I can extend the comfort he needs. When he's broken and hurting, allow me to appreciate what he's feeling so I can be part of the healing process. Remind me turn to You to support and care for him in every way. Please, Lord, teach me how to intercede for him when he finds it difficult to pray. When tears flow, please help me to be there to do whatever is necessary to bring him comfort. Lord, fill me with compassion for my husband. Thank You for the incredible blessing of loving this man so much that when he hurts, I hurt too.

Thank You, Lord, for _____'s heart—not only for me, but for You. I pray that through reading Your Word and spending time with You, he would gain a greater capacity to extend love, comfort, and compassion to every life he touches. That by Your strength and power, he would be a man who loves people well, especially when it's hardest to do so. I pray that his ability to extend compassion and to care for and comfort me when I need it most would continue to grow throughout our life together.

Lord, teach _____ and me to carry each other's burdens. When hard times come, help us persevere with compassion and comfort toward each other in the midst of every challenge. Help us to extend grace when needed—teach us to be quick to forgive, to respond with deep sensitivity, tenderness, and appreciation for each other. Through the comfort You pour into our lives, may we continuously learn how to better comfort one another. Help us to encourage and build one another up, because the world, the flesh, and the devil ever strive to tear us down.

Lord Jesus, thank You for being the perfect example. We only need to look to You and Your life to know how to live. You never compromised Your character to live a life filled with compassion. Give us deep insight and discernment so we can live that kind of life. Help us seek You in order to recognize each other's needs before they are even spoken. And give us the wisdom to pray accordingly and strategically. O Lord, may the comfort and compassion we extend to each other and others be a witness to Your presence in our lives—so much so that people would reach out to us in times of great need. I pray, Lord, that because of Christ's compassion and comfort working in and through us, we would be a beacon of hope in a world filled with hurting people.

In Jesus's name, amen.

* *

The Lord is gracious and righteous; our God is full of compassion.
The Lord protects the unwary; when I was brought low, he saved me.
PSALM 116:5-6

I have told you these things, so that in me you may have peace.
In this world you will have trouble.
But take heart! I have overcome the world.
JOHN 16:33

Challenge #4

This is going to be fun! When you have time over the next few days, make a list of the top twelve reasons why you love your fiancé. After you've finished, put it in an envelope and seal it. The plan is to give your fiancé the envelope on your honeymoon. Get creative and have fun with this.

Maybe you want to sneak it into his suitcase, hide it under his pillow, or hand it to him when you're out to dinner one night. Use your imagination! It's good to get into the habit of reminding him—and yourself—why you love each other so much. In fact, you may even want to put a reminder or two into your planner or on your phone calendar to ensure that you periodically remember why you want to spend the rest of your life with this man.

*M*y mom and I always joke that she's a "recovering control freak." Since I am her daughter, we think it might actually be hereditary. It's like a sub-conscious life skill—we go through life trying to control everything without even realizing that our need to control has begun to control us.

When it came to planning the most important day of my life, this part of me went into hyperdrive. Trust me, you *don't* want to get in the way of my mom and me trying to make something wedding-related happen!

My mom wanted to be involved in the entire wedding planning process, and honestly, I wanted her to be more involved than she already was! Some of you may feel the same way. You consult your mom for all the little day-in-and-day-out life details that only a mom could understand. She's your number one go-to, though sometimes you have to finesse your way through a bit of panic, a few tears, and just a touch of irrationality—but it's part of her charm and can be downright endearing.

Others of you may not have a good relationship with your mom, or you might want to pull your hair out every time she brings up color schemes or how she thinks the centerpieces should look. I get it, it's *your* wedding. You want to be in control.

So here's a word of advice: let the mother of the bride be exactly that: the *mother* of the bride. It is *your* wedding, and it should be exactly how you've always dreamed it would be. But God has placed amazing people in your life for advice, counsel, prayer, and to tell you when your hair looks like a mess or the wedding dress you just tried on does not do a thing for your figure. Whether that person is your mom, grandma, or best friend, confide in them with all your crazy unknowns. Allow them to play a specific and special role during this amazing journey. You're not meant to do it all on your own. You'll drive yourself and everyone around you crazy if you try to handle all the details and demands without help.

Along the way, if you find yourself really annoyed with your mom or whoever, pray first and then kindly remind them that you appreciate their help and want them to be a part of the process, but this is your wedding and you will make the decisions. Being upfront, honest, and kind is always the best way to go.

Ultimately, we want to be in control so that nothing in life feels out of control. Oftentimes the things that are out of our control are what drive us to give complete control to the One who holds all things together. I need to be reminded daily of this truth, but especially during wedding planning. You will try your hardest to make everything perfect, not only for you but for your guests too. But don't get so busy in the details that you lose sight of why you're getting married in the first place. Marriage is God's gift to you and your husband. Let the Lord take control—He's much better at it than we are!

FRUIT OF THE SPIRIT

Dear Lord,

I praise You for who _____ is because of who You are. Thank You for starting a good work in his life and making him the man he is today. I pray that Your Holy Spirit would daily lead and transform him in such a way that the fruit of the Spirit is undeniable in his life.

Because of Your Spirit, Your power and presence are always at work within us. Your presence fills us with love, joy, peace, patience, kindness, goodness, faithfulness, gentleness, and self-control. Thank You, Holy Spirit.

Lord, I pray that my fiancé would experience deep love through You, through me, and in our marriage. Let Your love be what motivates him to love me the way You want him to. And, Lord, I pray that I would fiercely love my husband with all the love You have so graciously given me. Help us to daily die to ourselves so that we can put one another first. But most importantly, Lord, I pray that our love for You would always be greater than our love for each other.

Dear God, I pray that my soon-to-be spouse would overflow with great joy. No matter where he goes or what circumstance he finds himself in, I pray that people would want the joy they see in _____, just by being in his presence. When times are hard and he is broken within, give him a supernatural joy that pierces through the darkest circumstances. Lord, bless me with the gift of bringing my husband-to-be extraordinary joy—joy that no other human can give him.

Make him a man filled with Your perfect peace. May he be slow to anger and rich in love (James 1:19). When life gets hectic and confusing, I pray Your peace will reign in him. Remind him where true, everlasting peace comes from when he forgets. Lord, in our marriage, no matter what obstacles and trials we face, please give us Your perfect peace that surpasses all understanding to guard our hearts and minds in Christ (Philippians 4:7).

Lord, teach _____ to be patient and to wait on You. Help him to rest in Your perfect timing and provision. Remind him that You work all things together for good for those who love You and are called according to Your purpose (Romans 8:28). Lord, help us to be patient with one another, and to think and pray before we speak.

I pray that my beloved would always be kind, especially when it's hard—not just kind to me, but to everyone around him. Lord, when it would be easy for me to get frustrated and annoyed with him, help me to speak to him with kindness, love, and respect. Similarly, let him display gentleness through his affection, influence, and power. I pray that _____ would tenderly care for me all the days of his life.

Father, I pray that goodness would flow out of my husband-to-be's life. May our lives together reflect the goodness of who You are, and may we never cease to declare the goodness of Your majesty!

O Lord, may this precious man of God remain faithful all the days of his life. Help him to remain faithful and obedient to Your Word. Help him to be faithful to me and our marriage and faithful to the words he speaks as well. May he mean every word that he says and follow through on the promises he makes. Most importantly, help _____ to remain faithful to You—to what You have called him to do and who You have called him to be. I pray that we would never waver in the vows we make to each other on our wedding day. Let the integrity of heart and faithfulness we currently possess remain at the core of our marriage for the rest of our lives.

Lastly, Lord, I pray that self-control would be deeply rooted within his heart. May he always let Your Holy Spirit lead and control every area of his life. Lord, when people see us, let them see You by the way the fruit of the Spirit pours out of our lives.

In Jesus's name, amen.

. . . .

But the fruit of the Spirit is love, joy, peace, forbearance,
kindness, goodness, faithfulness, gentleness and self-control.
Against such things there is no law.

GALATIANS 5:22–23

Remain in me, as I also remain in you.
No branch can bear fruit by itself; it must remain in the vine.
Neither can you bear fruit unless you remain in me.

JOHN 15:4

Live a life worthy of the Lord and please him in every way:
bearing fruit in every good work [and] growing in the knowledge of God.

COLOSSIANS 1:10

Lord Jesus,

I don't know how many days You have determined for me to live here on earth. I don't know how long I have to serve You and love others as I pass through time. But I do know that I never want to take one moment, one heartbeat, one breath for granted—I want to celebrate Your love and faithfulness all the days of my life.

Whether we realize it or not, life is short no matter how long we live. Tomorrow is never guaranteed to anyone. Each one of us has but a vapor of time to make an eternal difference. Lord, please keep me and _____ mindful that life is but a breath that appears for a little while and then vanishes (James 4:14). Please help us make every moment matter for eternity.

Lord, I pray that my fiancé and I would share the same eternal values. May we never be tempted by the empty glamour of worldly promises, but instead remember that what is seen is temporary and what is unseen is eternal. Father, may we both commit wholeheartedly to Your will so that the things we do in time last forever. Help us live out the reality that our forefathers in the faith lived out in Hebrews 11:13, and walk as "foreigners and strangers on earth." Lord, please help us long for the joy, beauty, and perfection of our heavenly home, just as they did. May we live with an eternal mindset and always keep our focus on You and Your kingdom.

Father, You are not bound by time, You created it. You knew exactly how many hours we would need each day. We all have the same twenty-four hours to serve You and impact the world! The truth is, all we can take with us when we leave is what we've done with our time. Every day is one day closer to eternity. Lord, please give _____ and me wisdom and understanding to use the time You have given us to honor and serve You.

Lord, I don't want us to waste a single moment. Mold and shape us to see life through a forever lens. Remind us when we get caught up in the day-to-day cares and concerns that everything we do and are in this moment will impact forever.

Because of that, I pray You would keep our hearts and minds set on eternity. Please help us use the earthly things that pass away to establish that which can never fade or perish. Help our minds, motives, and desires be rooted in Your kingdom here and beyond time so that what we do in time endures forever. Please anchor our hopes and dreams in Your will so that we choose to use every moment for Your glory. Thank You, Lord!

In Jesus's name, amen.

* *

There is a time for everything, and a season
for every activity under the heavens.
ECCLESIASTES 3:1

Since you call on a Father who judges each person's work impartially,
live out your time as foreigners here in reverent fear.
1 PETER 1:17

Let us not become weary in doing good, for at the proper time
we will reap a harvest if we do not give up.
GALATIANS 6:9

Lord,

As I prepare my heart and mind to become a wife, I also pray that You would prepare my body to belong to my husband. What a beautiful picture of surrender, holiness, and purity this is, to become completely one with my husband, physically and spiritually.

Lord, You created a man and a woman to become physically one through marriage. Sex is a gift created to be holy and sacrificial. Lord, thank You that soon _____ and I will become one flesh. Heavenly Father, please honor, bless, and protect this very significant part of our marriage. Thank You that in the context and holiness of marriage, You bless sexual intercourse. It is designed to be sacred, a picture of Christ and His love for the church. Thank You for sex! Please prepare us daily to live as one both spiritually and physically. Keep our hearts, minds, and bodies pure before You and one another.

Thank You for choosing _____ for me to love and cherish the rest of my life. When we are married, my body will be his, and his will be mine. Please help us to be comfortable and confident with the bodies You have given us. Lord, if there is any part of _____'s body that he is afraid to share with me, please set him free. And please do the same for me, Lord. I pray that we will forever cherish the gift that our bodies are to each other and use this sacred gift as You have intended for us to use it. Thank You for this lasting covenant and physical bond of oneness.

Lord, I pray that we would have a lifelong affection for one another and that we would freely and openly display this affection through how we treat each other. Dear God, help me to know how to show love to _____ in the way that he needs to receive it, and help him know how to show me love and affection as well. Lord, may we always enjoy and never take for granted the gift of a long hug and gentle kiss on the cheek.

Men are visual. You made them this way, Lord. So, please protect _____'s eyes, the windows to his soul. I pray that his eyes would long to see me and only me. Please keep his heart and mind pure and free from sexual temptations of any form. And I pray that my heart would always desire my husband. Please help us to remain physically and emotionally attracted to each other as we grow deeper and deeper in love. Thank You, Lord.

In Jesus's name, amen.

. . . .

That is why a man leaves his father and mother
and is united to his wife, and they become one flesh.
GENESIS 2:24

Like an apple tree among the trees of the forest is my beloved
among the young men. I delight to sit in his shade,
and his fruit is sweet to my taste.
SONG OF SOLOMON 2:3

A wife of noble character who can find? She is worth far more than rubies.
Her husband has full confidence in her and lacks nothing of value.
PROVERBS 31:10-11

Dear God,

We live in a fallen world filled with sickness, disease, and death; yet You have graciously provided everything we need to survive. Good health is a gift. Please help _____ and me to appreciate the good health You have given us and use it to accomplish Your will. God, may we never take our health for granted. Instead, teach us to appreciate what we have been given moment by moment, day by day.

Lord, a healthy lifestyle can be maintained in many ways, ways that take time, effort, balance, and wisdom. Exercise and eating right are essential. Help us to also be vigilant in staying well informed and educated so we make good health decisions and precautions. Teach me and _____ to prioritize our daily schedules. Bless us with a godly, balanced perspective so we can appropriately focus on our physical, emotional, and spiritual health.

When sickness and health issues arise, whether simple colds or life-threatening illnesses, please remind us that You are sovereign and good. You are the miracle maker, and You still perform miracles today. Give me and _____ patience, tenderness, and empathy as we walk alongside each other through sickness and health. Help us each to be strong when the other is weak; to come boldly to You in prayer asking for divine healing and provision. Teach us to reach out to each other in the most practical ways with hearts filled with compassion.

Although You have provided doctors, medications, machines, and various other medical interventions, You are and always will be the ultimate healer. Help us to seek You, the Healer, daily for our overall health needs and well-being. There are many ways to get sick in this fallen world, so please, Father, help us to respect and appreciate our health while trusting You so we don't live in fear.

Lord, our health is more than physical—mental, emotional, and spiritual health are just as vital. Transform us by the renewing of our minds. Keep Your truth ever before us and help us hide Your Word in our hearts so that we will not sin against You. Pour Your truth into our hearts so we can walk by faith and not by sight. Father, keep us from getting caught up in the cares of this world. Help us to focus on whatever is true, noble, praiseworthy, and excellent—to fix our eyes on Jesus, the author and perfecter of our faith. Please give _____ and me lives that are balanced and healthy, mentally, emotionally, and spiritually.

Our spiritual health is vital to living a life that honors You, Lord. _____ and I desperately need Your grace and mercy in this area of our lives. Without a strong, vibrant spirit in deep fellowship with You, how can we love You, walk in obedience, or share Your love with a perishing world? God, please give us the resolve to maintain a diligent study of Your Word and to persist in prayer. Keep praise and thanksgiving on our lips and help us trust You to act on our behalf. I pray that our spiritual health would be evident through our love and commitment to each other, but more importantly to You.

Dear Lord, please protect us! Shield us from the battle that rages against our flesh and spirit. Help us seek Your wisdom and guidance in every aspect of our health—physical, emotional, mental, and spiritual—so we can live for You and love You with all our heart, mind, soul, and strength.

In Jesus's name, amen.

. . . .

Heal me, LORD, and I will be healed;
save me and I will be saved, for you are the one I praise.
JEREMIAH 17:14

SUFFERING
AND TRIALS

Heavenly Father,

Our greatest need has always been and will always be You. There is so much pain, suffering, and heartbreak in this broken world. You know the reasons why; You see the end and every moment in between. Your heart must be filled with sorrow for Your children. Lord, You've told us to expect troubles in this world, and part of following You is enduring suffering and hardship. However, I'm reminded that You endured the greatest suffering imaginable— and because of that, I have a place to run with my sorrow and grief. Because of You, I have hope. Because You have overcome the world, I too can overcome.

We need You, Lord. _____ and I need You. You are everything we need during seasons of suffering. Trials will come and go in life and in marriage. Life, commitment, and sacrificial love will not always be easy. However, You are still God, and You are still good. Lord, as we walk through trials together, help us look to You for guidance, strength, and comfort. Remind us that the things of this world will never satisfy. Please give us the reassurance we need to know that You are holding every part of our lives in Your mighty hands. When circumstances don't make sense, help us cling to the truth that Your plans are far greater and more meaningful than our own. Remind us that Your ways and thoughts are higher than ours. You see and know the unknown—please help us to trust You when we can't see the road ahead. During seasons of pain, humble us and strengthen our walk with You.

Whether it's struggles in our marriage or in our family, Father, remind _____ and me that You fight for us. Thank You, Lord! We are powerless in and of our own strength. We need You to fight the battles we were never meant to fight in the first place. We need Your comfort so that we can, in turn, comfort others who are suffering. Thank You in advance for what You will do in and through my fiancé and me amid life's many heartbreaks and trials.

Lord, I pray that You will strengthen our marriage through the sufferings we face. I pray that the trials and tragedies _____ and I walk through would only make us love You and each other more. Use them to increase our confidence in You and Your unwavering mercy. Help us depend on You and Your perfect provision and protection. When we fall, help us to pick each other back up. When one of us hurts, help the other to be a source of gentleness and comfort. Help us to always lean on each other, and ultimately together depend fully on Your strength.

You are sovereign. You are good. Let us never lose sight of who You are, in the midst of our suffering. Thank You, Lord.

In Jesus's mighty name I pray, amen.

· ·

And the God of all grace, who called you to his eternal glory in Christ,
after you have suffered a little while, will himself restore you
and make you strong, firm and steadfast.
1 PETER 5:10

We . . . glory in our sufferings,
because we know that suffering produces perseverance;
perseverance, character; and character, hope.
ROMANS 5:3–4

This next assignment is strictly for you! Again, break out the pen and notebook and get ready to write. Make a list of a dozen ways you want to bless your husband during the first year of your marriage. Search your heart and think about things that your fiancé loves—things that will bring him closer to Christ, things that he loves to do. These can be as personal and intimate as a quiet night for two at home with the phone off and no distractions, a fishing or hunting outing, or a day for him to go golfing with the boys or maybe catch an NFL football game. You craft these, not just based on what you know about him, but on how well you know him. This way, once a month, you can share your love for him in a fun, meaningful way.

$\mathcal{B}$elieve it or not, wedding shoes are a big deal. I don't know if this comes as a shock to you, but I had no idea what I was in for when I started shopping around for the perfect shoe to complement my dress. The thing is, no one sees your shoes unless, of course, your dress is shorter than most wedding dresses. From the moment you put them on, the one person that will appreciate your wedding shoes the most is you. So they'd better be awesome, and they'd better be comfortable.

Let's be honest, most high heels or stilettos are not comfortable. In fact, wearing two-inch heels or higher is nothing short of a workout and somewhat dangerous if you're not used to walking in them. Not only that, like your wedding dress, you will more than likely wear your wedding shoes only on your wedding day. Even so, they have to be spectacular because they'll be part of the overall beautiful you on the most amazing day of your life.

My husband-to-be is six feet six, so I'll be wearing the highest heels I can handle without falling flat on my face or breaking my ankle. Confession time: I have wide feet, so most of the designer wedding shoes didn't work for me. Trust me, I have tried to squeeze my foot into every style of Christian Louboutin heel on the market. Not happening.

Whether you're looking for a four-inch heel or prefer a more casual and comfortable bohemian-style shoe, I suggest you start wearing your wedding shoes as often as possible (without getting them dirty) at least a month before the wedding. You'll want to break in your shoes and let them adjust to your feet. No one wants blisters on their wedding day.

Whatever shoes you end up selecting, don't forget to wear them as often as you can before the big day. You're going to look amazing!

Fun fact . . . for our wedding reception, instead of doing the traditional garter and bouquet throw, we decided to do something different. We had everyone clear the dance floor and then placed some chairs in a straight line in the center of the room. My bridesmaids and I then sat on the row of chairs. After we were seated, my husband (sounds so weird saying that) and our grooms-men came out onto the dance floor with boxes. Inside each box was a pair of sneakers. The guys knelt down, took off our shoes, and put on our sneakers. And then we all danced together and invited our guests back out onto the dance floor to do the same. It was so much fun! I would have danced all night with my wedding shoes on, but wearing sneakers was way more comfortable.

Dear God,

No one is immune from danger, heartbreak, and tragedy in this life. We see and hear about it every time we turn on the television or scroll through social media. It's evident that the forces of darkness are at work. And yet, You rule and reign over all. You're still on Your throne! The perfect plan You set in motion from the beginning of time is moving forward, just as You promised it would. No matter what is going on in the world, we can trust You to take care of us and be with us as we go through life.

Thank You for promising to meet all our needs (Philippians 4:19), whether we need the grace to endure to the end, triumph through the unthinkable, or help in keeping a godly perspective in the face of deep heartbreak. Lord, help _____ and me to never forget that Your protection and provision are promised no matter how severe the trials. You are greater than any set of circumstances no matter how desperate they seem.

Lord, I pray that You would not only protect us physically, but that You would guard our hearts as well. Keep our hearts set on You. I pray that we would be diligent in guarding each other's hearts and treating one another the way You have called us to. Thank You that no matter what may come against us, what You have brought together, no one and nothing can tear apart.

Father, You have promised to provide for us—we're worth more than the birds of the air, which You care for every day. Because You are faithful, we are encouraged not to "worry about your life, what you will eat or drink; or about your body, what you will wear. Is not life more than food, and the body more than clothes?" (Matthew 6:25). Lord, I ask that You would help us to trust You to provide our needs. Help us look at our circumstances in light of Your perfect promises and provision. Even when everything seems to be falling apart, remind us that You hold everything together.

I pray that _____ and I would cling to the unwavering truth that You are a good Father. You know exactly what we need, when we need it, and You will be faithful to provide exactly what we need in Your perfect timing. Keep us from wanting more than we need and help us lay up treasures in heaven that never lose their value.

I pray, Lord, that we will seek first Your kingdom and Your righteousness because You have assured us that if we do, everything else will be given to us as well. Father, help us to live for eternity and trust You with all that we are and have as we walk through time. Life is so much more than provision, and what we need is so much more than just material. We need emotional provision, spiritual provision, and we need wisdom to make day-to-day decisions. Please pour Your grace into our lives—the grace to seek You and Your will above and beyond all material desires.

I also pray for Your protection through our pursuit of Your will. In Luke 17:33, You tell us that we need to lose our lives to preserve them, and yet that is not the world's way. So I ask that, when everything around us pressures us to give in to the temptations to go our own way, You would give us the determination and conviction to lay down our lives. I pray for daily strength for my fiancé and me as we choose to follow You one day at a time. Help us to put You before everything and to love You more than our own lives. As we give ourselves to You, You've promised to provide all the protection and provision we need. Thank You, Lord!

In Jesus's name, amen.

. . . .

The LORD himself goes before you and will be with you; he will never leave you nor forsake you. Do not be afraid; do not be discouraged.

DEUTERONOMY 31:8

Dear Lord,

You are for us! Thank You that we already have victory in You. Thank You for sending Your Son, Jesus. The battle waged against us was won when He died on the cross and rose from the grave. He not only defeated death and the enemy, but every other weapon that will try to form against us. Thank You, Lord!

Please help _____ and me to live in the knowledge of our victory through Christ. May there be a confidence and security to our demeanor that reveals the triumph of a war already won. Let us never forget that the battle is not against flesh and blood (Ephesians 6:12). Keep us from trying to take matters into our own hands; instead, help us to entrust it all to You, remembering that the battle is Yours—not ours. When life becomes hard and seems hopeless, remind us that our triumph is guaranteed through Yours.

There is no failure or defeat for those who are in Christ. Though circumstances may cause us to feel as though we've been buried beneath the weight of the world, You are doing a work in us, forming the image of Your Son in our hearts. You are preparing us to rise from the dust of defeat with a greater sense of victory and purpose!

Lord, remind _____ that the battle is Yours. When trials and hardships come, help him to take up the armor that You've equipped him with. Hide Your Word deep in his heart so he will not sin against You. Protect him from the evil one and the temptations that lurk around every corner. I pray that he would not buy in to the world, the flesh, or the devil's deceitful schemes, but always choose You, no matter the cost.

God, please remind _____ that he has an unshakeable victory in You that cannot be taken from him. He is saved by grace and sealed with the promised Holy Spirit. Nothing in this world can thwart the plans that You have for his life. Help my future husband to live and walk in complete freedom, knowing that he is Yours and the enemy is a liar. There's nothing that can hold him back from giving all he has to the purpose of Your kingdom. When he feels defeated, remind him that he is an heir to the throne of the King of kings, and nothing can defeat those whom God has chosen.

Heavenly Father, please guard and protect our relationship as we prepare for the wedding. Help us to fix our eyes on Jesus and trust You to prepare our hearts for the covenant of marriage. Please remind us that victory comes through Christ, so that even in the midst of trials, we can live victoriously. Lord, help us to battle in prayer every day for each other. The enemy cannot stand against us, especially when we stand firm in Your Word—together. Lord, don't allow _____ and me to ever cease praying for each other, knowing that You've gone before us and paid the ultimate price for our victory.

Lord, help us surrender to You. You've defeated fear and failure. You've defeated pain and suffering. You've defeated death. You won, and because of that, we stand with You—victorious! Remind us that because You are God and we are Yours, we are and always will be victorious. You have called us out of the darkness into Your glorious light. Help us never forget that we are children of the King. In this world we will have struggles, but You have overcome the world. Therefore, we are more than conquerors, and in Christ, we are overcomers!

In Jesus's name, amen.

. . . .

But thanks be to God! He gives us the victory through our Lord Jesus Christ.
1 CORINTHIANS 15:57

Dear God,

You tell us in Psalm 127:3 that "children are a heritage from the LORD, offspring a reward from him." I pray that _____ and I would share in this precious reward from You, Father, and that You would bless us with children. How great is the responsibility unique to raising children; the sacrifice, wisdom, hard work, and selflessness that are required to be good, godly parents. And yet, Lord, the investment brings a remarkable return and treasure beyond comprehension. I don't know when the time will come for _____ and me to have children, but I trust in Your perfect timing. You are sovereign. You alone are the Author of life. So I trust that, even now, You will graciously prepare us for this incredible blessing.

As You prepare me to be a wife, Lord, prepare me to be a God-fearing mom as well. Prepare my fiancé to be a God-fearing father. My greatest prayer is that, as parents, we would love and obey You and point our children to the truth. And as a result, Father, I pray they would love Jesus and follow Him all the days of their lives. Help me to always show our children love, grace, and compassion. I pray that _____ would be a godly man who would display loyalty, forgiveness, and courage. Lord, when our children look at me and their dad, I pray that they would see You.

Please help us to live what we believe and teach our children by example. I pray that as parents, we would speak life and love over our children; that they would know patience, sincerity, and godliness by the way their father and I treat each other. Lord, protect us from hypocrisy and from compromising our integrity. Help us to seek You for guidance and wisdom as we parent and love our children unconditionally. Help us remember that little eyes see when we're not looking and little ears hear, even when we whisper. Please let us always be willing to work hard to provide, discipline without criticism give sincere approval and, as needed, loving correction. Help us to always forgive, be fair, and respectful.

Heavenly Father, please prepare our home for children even now. Prepare our hearts and minds to be parents. Help us to love You deeply, and to love each other the same, so that we can display Your love to our children. Thank You in advance for what You will do in and through our family. Be magnified and glorified, Lord! I pray that our family would greatly impact Your kingdom and that our godly marriage would be an example for our children and for many generations to come.

Thank You for the gift of children and for bringing _____ and me together so that we might bring forth new life.

In Jesus's name, amen.

. . . .

He took the children in his arms,
placed his hands on them and blessed them.
MARK 10:16

Children, obey your parents in the Lord, for this is right.
"Honor your father and mother"—which is the first commandment with
a promise—"so that it may go well with you and that you may enjoy
long life on the earth." Fathers, do not exasperate your children;
instead, bring them up in the training and instruction of the Lord.
EPHESIANS 6:1-4

Dear Lord,

I am mindful of the fact that we all leave a legacy, either godly and virtuous or worldly and selfish. Thank You, God, that I can invest in eternity and by Your Spirit leave a legacy that will endure beyond the end of time. Father, I am a woman of God, and as such, I long to model my life after the person You describe in Proverbs 31:10–31. Protect me from my own selfish ambitions, from the world, the flesh, and the devil. Help me walk humbly before You so that everything I do and leave behind honors You.

God, I pray that my life and faith would point to Your awesome works. Help me live and love like Jesus. Help me be Your hands and feet, especially in my home. Help me love like You love and serve like You serve. Help me be obedient and bold in my faith, and let my husband and children see You at work as I step out in faith to live wholeheartedly for You. May _____ and I live in such a way that our children would experience You in their day-to-day lives through the reality of Your presence in our lives.

I pray for my future husband, that he would be mindful of every step he takes and the lasting repercussions his choices will have. I ask that he would remember Psalm 145:4 in his daily walk. Remind him that "one generation commends your works to another, they tell of your mighty acts." Help him live as an encouraging example to our family, friends, acquaintances, and strangers. I pray that his life would be a living testimony to who You are. I pray that our children would look up to their dad as the spiritual leader of our home and that they would seek him daily for godly wisdom and guidance.

Dear Father, help _____ and me to unreservedly pour out our lives, laying up treasures in heaven rather than on earth. When our time on earth has been fulfilled, I pray the opinions, perspectives, and views others have formed toward us as a couple all point to You. May our good works bring honor and glory to You alone. I pray that we would be ever mindful of the legacy we are leaving with each decision we make, every dollar we spend, and all the energy we invest. Lord, please let our choices and decisions be guided by how they will bless You and conform to Your will. Help us seek Your plan for our lives; never let the *good* undermine the *perfect* will of God. Above all, Lord, I pray that it would be our radical love that leaves the greatest legacy, revealing who You are and what You've accomplished in and through our lives.

Dear Lord, what has the greatest impact in life is usually caught rather than taught. And so I pray that _____ and I would lead lives that exemplify Your character and presence in our lives. Help us to walk in Your love in such a way that we live out Psalm 103:17, "But from everlasting to everlasting the *Lord's* love is with those who fear him, and his righteousness with their children's children." As our children and their children experience the wonder of Your love and goodness, may it be said of both of us, "well done, good and faithful servants."

In Jesus's name, amen.

. . . .

His master replied, "Well done, good and faithful servant!
You have been faithful with a few things;
I will put you in charge of many things.
Come and share your master's happiness!"
MATTHEW 25:23

PEACE

Lord,

You are the Prince of Peace! Apart from Your presence in our lives and Your sovereignty over all creation, we cannot experience peace. We live in a fallen world filled with darkness and turmoil. We want what we can't have and neglect to appreciate what we do have. We seek hope, healing, and peace in all the wrong places. Rescue us, Lord! Please forgive us. We need You.

Thank You that _____ and I can run to You with our troubled hearts and count on Your protection and perfect peace. Because of who You are, we have nothing to fear. Lord, I pray that Your peace, which transcends all understanding, would guard our hearts and minds in Christ Jesus (Philippians 4:7). Please help us to trust You with every single detail of our lives. As we prepare for our wedding day and life together, so much remains unknown. However, there's one thing we can be sure of—Your presence and peace will never leave us.

Heavenly Father, as _____ prepares his heart to be my husband, please draw him closer to Your heart. If he is struggling with something that I am unaware of, please show me how I can intercede for him and help him. Lord, if something or someone is causing _____ to be restless, anxious, or fearful, please help him to seek You for guidance, comfort, and peace.

_____ will be the man and leader of our home; help me to encourage and build him up in every area of his life. Lord, help me to place my expectations on Christ instead of heaping them on my fiancé. Please fill me with Your presence so that when _____ is wrestling with an issue in his life, I will be able to model for him Your overwhelming peace. Regardless of the worries or fears that may arise, when he is with me, please allow him to feel safe.

Your Word says that as one body, the church, we are called to peace (Colossians 3:15). This same truth applies to being one in marriage. Lord, when life gets hectic and being married gets hard, please remind us that You are God and You've got it all figured out. Nothing and no one can change Your sovereign plan for our lives. Heavenly Father, help us to let go of anything that would draw us away from You and Your perfect peace.

In every moment, help us to trust and depend on You, especially as we prepare for our wedding. Help us to focus on the beauty and purpose of marriage, rather than worry about all the details. But I also pray that You would orchestrate every detail for this incredible day. In our marriage, help us to depend on You and trust that You will always be with us to guide us throughout our entire lives.

Lord, thank You for everlasting peace!

In Jesus's name, amen.

. . . .

Peace I leave with you; my peace I give you.
I do not give to you as the world gives.
Do not let your hearts be troubled and do not be afraid.
JOHN 14:27

Let the peace of Christ rule in your hearts, since as members
of one body you were called to peace. And be thankful.
COLOSSIANS 3:15

For the last challenge, I want to share a deep truth that God revealed to me during what has been perhaps the most difficult season of my life. Over the past five years, I have watched and helped my mom take care of my dad through three bouts of squamous cell carcinoma—oral cancer. During his second battle, the doctors gave him a 10 percent chance of survival. It is nothing short of a miracle that my dad was present to walk me down the aisle on my wedding day.

But it was during my father's battle with cancer that I gained a deeper passion and longing for God. I also learned what a blessing it is to take care of someone, to give of yourself without expecting anything in return. I desperately wanted and prayed for healing for my dad, but the whole while, I was learning to want the Healer more. Rather than pray for the rest that God could give my dad, I learned to pray that my father would want Jesus more than anything else—the Giver more than the gift.

This is the heart of challenge #6—the Giver, the gift, and the giving.

One of the many decisions you will make during the wedding planning process is whether to give favors to your guests at the reception. Parker and I decided that rather than give favors, we would give back instead. On your wedding day, your guests will bless you with gifts—gifts you've likely registered for at various stores. (By the way, how fun is doing the wedding gift registry? Parker and I had so much fun, and I suppose we went a little over-board. It's hard not to when you get to pick out whatever you want.)

Back to my challenge. Have you considered blessing your guests through giving back rather than giving a gift? A wedding favor is great, but after your wedding, the favor stops giving. How about giving a gift that never stops giving by investing in a charity or ministry? Parker and I chose to give to my family's foundation—Hunter's Hope.

Ultimately, this must be a decision that you and your husband-to-be make together. It is such a beautiful way to start off your marriage. The amount you choose isn't what matters. No matter how much or how little you give, it's the heart and the act of giving that is the greatest blessing! At the end of the day, you will always be more blessed through giving than receiving.

The Wedding—it's full of excitement, joy, anticipation, and so much more. It will be one of the fastest, craziest, most amazing, and blessed days of your life. You will never forget this day! The moments you share celebrating with your new husband, family, and friends will be indelibly marked on your memory. I am so excited for you. And I am praying for you. Yes, you! My mom and I have prayed for every bride and mother of the bride who will read this book. And it has been an honor and a privilege to do so.

So, I want to share with you one final tip, an extra-special something that my husband and I did the morning of our wedding day. Like many wedding couples, we decided beforehand that we wanted to give each other a gift to open just before the ceremony. We chose not to do the "first look" because we wanted to wait to see each other for the first time at the altar. So, in order to give our gifts before the ceremony, we had them delivered to each other at the church.

Little did Parker know that I had been planning and creating his gift before we even met. When I was thirteen years old, I started writing love letters and keeping a journal for my future husband. I did not know his name or anything about him, but God did. And so I prayed and wrote down everything my heart longed to tell him. Wrapped in a wooden box were countless letters and prayers that I had been writing since I was a little girl. Love letters to my future husband. Prayers for the man I'd always loved but didn't know until God brought him to me.

I also gave Parker something else . . . something just as significant and precious to me; another gift I had been holding on to since I was thirteen—my purity ring. The box that had held my wedding band now held my purity ring. And the finger that had once worn a little girl's purity ring, symbolizing her commitment to God and her future husband, would soon wear a wedding ring. Attached to the box, I wrote a note: "This is for you to give our daughter someday." I am getting overwhelmed all over again just telling you about it. God is amazing!

Love. It's the gift that keeps on giving. God's love . . . the greatest gift! My husband will have those love letters forever. He can look back and see how God was preparing my heart for him and our hearts and lives for each other all along. And the ring . . . maybe one day, Parker will give my purity ring to our daughter. Wow! God is so good!

So I encourage you—plan to give each other something special on your wedding day. As I stated, Parker and I chose not to see each other before the ceremony, although we did pray together moments before we went into the church sanctuary. Whether you choose to give your gifts in person or through a friend, make time to give a gift to each other. Trust me, you'll cherish them forever.

Your gift to your husband will look very different than mine. Give what is deeply meaningful and special to you and your relationship. No matter how big or how small. Maybe you have a letter your fiancé wrote to you while you were dating. Or maybe you took a screenshot from your phone of your first text conversation. Either of these would be very meaningful gifts. Pray about it and ask God to show you what to do. Whatever you decide, it will be perfect.

Side note: I would also encourage you and your fiancé to pray together before the ceremony. If you decide to do a first look, take some time to be still and pray. If not, do what we did—get a blindfold or hide around the corner. Do whatever you have to do to make it happen. God is the glory of your marriage—make time to come to Him together before you become one.

THE WEDDING

(Quick note: The next few prayers are specific to the actual wedding day. Depending on what time the wedding ceremony is, you might want to read these the night before, or a few days before the wedding. It's up to you. Can you believe the big day is finally here? I'm so excited for you. I'm praying for you.)

Lord,

This is the day that You have made! Thank You! I am so excited! After all the praying and planning, my wedding day is finally here. I have been dreaming and praying about this day since I was a little girl. Imagining how I will look in my beautiful wedding dress and veil, walking down the aisle with my dad to meet my groom, sharing handwritten vows filled with all my heart's desires for my husband, and celebrating with those who mean the most to us.

Heavenly Father, as You know, I have been praying for the man You chose for me, the one I will spend the rest of my life with. Today, I am believing and praying that the love You have given us will set our wedding day apart, revealing Your outrageous love to everyone celebrating with us.

Lord, before I was born, You orchestrated every detail in my life to bring me to this moment. You have been strategically and purposefully preparing my heart, mind, and body in every way. Heavenly Father, help me be keenly aware of Your presence today. Fill me to overflowing with Your love so that nothing and no one can steal my joy. Help me be fully present so I can take it all in and enjoy and appreciate every moment. Please protect my mind and heart from distractions so that I can fully receive every blessing You have prepared for me today.

Lord, my heart's desire is that I would radiate the beauty of who You are with every step I take. When people see me, open their eyes so they can see a glimpse of You! Please let Your joy fill me—a joy that simply cannot be contained but spills over like flooding water.

When my groom sees me for the first time, I pray that it's Your radiance and glory he sees. May he know in that moment that I belong to You and have been set apart to love Jesus more than anything and because of that . . . I will love him unconditionally and wholeheartedly.

Heavenly Father, I thank You that the day I have prayed for is now here. I thank You, too, for giving me the man I have been praying for. Be glorified in and through us today.

For Your glory . . . in Jesus's name, amen.

· ·

A wife of noble character is her husband's crown.

PROVERBS 12:4

Find a good spouse, you find a good life—
and even more: the favor of GOD!

PROVERBS 18:22 MSG

Wives, submit yourselves to your own husbands, as you do to the Lord.
For the husband is the head of the wife as Christ is the head of the church,
his body, of which he is the Savior. Now as the church submits to Christ,
so also wives should submit to their husbands in everything.

EPHESIANS 5:22–24

Lord,

Wow, I am overwhelmed and in awe of You! You are so good to me. Thank You, Lord! My heart is so full. All I want to do is praise You and thank You! It's hard to even comprehend that right now, I'm praying for the man who will soon be my husband—the man You chose for me before time began. Thank You, Lord! Thank You that I get to call _____ my husband for the rest of our earthly lives. Thank You for choosing him. Out of all the people in this world, You chose _____ to be mine. It's amazing and so humbling to think that You love me so much that You'd give him to me.

Lord, You have entrusted me to love my husband for as long as we both shall live. Help me to love him the way You do. Help us never take the love You have so graciously given us for granted. Lord, please guard his heart and encourage him to pursue You above all else. Help him to love Jesus more than he loves me.

Just as You have prepared me for this day, You have also been preparing my groom. You have been at work in his life, molding him into the image of Christ. You created him and know him better than he knows himself. Lord, You have been preparing him to make the promises he will make today as he steps into the covenant of marriage. Thank You, Lord, that I can have confidence in You and all that You have accomplished in his life thus far to prepare him for a lifetime with me. I am so blessed!

On this day, I pray that _____ would feel the power of the Holy Spirit at work. Give him an overwhelming sense of Your love and presence. Remind him that You will never leave him or forsake him and that You live to intercede for him. Because of Your great love, he can experience and know real love. Remind him that, through Christ, You have given him everything he needs to be the godly husband You created him to be.

Please give my groom the peace Your Word speaks of—not the kind of peace the world offers but peace that surpasses all understanding. I pray that as he awaits his bride at the altar, he would feel overwhelmed with Your love . . . and mine. I pray that he would never forget the words and promises we speak in our vows today. Please remind him that marriage is an enduring covenant shaped by lifelong promises. Help him to be faithful and follow through on every promise he makes today. And help me do the same. Lord, what You have brought together, let no man tear apart.

Heavenly Father, I pray that _____ would radiate Your glory as he gives himself to me through the covenant of marriage. Thank You for blessing me with this amazing man . . . until death finally parts us.

All for Your glory . . . amen.

. . . .

Therefore what God has joined together, let no one separate.
MARK 10:9

Husbands, love your wives, just as Christ loved the church
and gave himself up for her. . . . In this same way,
husbands ought to love their wives as their own bodies.
He who loves his wife loves himself.
EPHESIANS 5:25, 28

Lord,

Family and friends are among the greatest blessings You have given us on earth. I cannot even imagine what my life would be like without the people You have placed in it. I absolutely believe that You have orchestrated all the details, at just the right time, so that the people You wanted in my circle of influence would be there for me. Lord, thank You for giving me and my fiancé amazing family members and friends. They are a testament to Your goodness and love for us. Our wedding day will be that much more special because of the family and friends here celebrating with us. Father, I am especially thankful that they will be here to witness Your love and all that You have done in our lives.

God, thank You for family members and friends who have been a valuable source of comfort and encouragement to us as we have prepared for the wedding. Thank You for those who have exemplified what godly, loving marriages should look like. Lord, I am grateful for all the people You have brought into our lives, but I am especially thankful for the family members and friends who have prayed for and encouraged us in our walk with You. They have been an inspiration and an example that we can emulate in our own marriage. Lord, I pray that the godly people You have placed in our lives would continue to pray for us long after the wedding is over.

Lord, please bless these family members and friends who are with us today. I pray that they would be encouraged by our joy and motivated by our passion, and that we would be a living example of Your love and goodness. Help us to invest in our family and friends and love them like You do. As they witness our vows and the sacredness of the covenant we are making in Your presence, I pray that they would be moved to want to know and love You more.

Heavenly Father, let our wedding day serve as an invitation to those who are not part of the greater, forever family—Your family! Please help _____ and me to represent You well. Thank You that, because of Jesus, we are heirs with Christ and members of a family and kingdom that will never be shaken. A family that will last for eternity. Lord, for our family and friends who don't know You, I pray that they would see You reflected in the way my husband and I love You and each other. Please stir hearts and draw people to Yourself through what they will experience during our wedding and reception.

Thank You for giving us the opportunity to be an example and an expression of how much You love Your children.

In Jesus's name, amen.

. . . .

I no longer call you servants, because a servant does not know
his master's business. Instead, I have called you friends, for everything
that I learned from my Father I have made known to you.

JOHN 15:15

The righteous choose their friends carefully,
but the way of the wicked leads them astray.

PROVERBS 12:26

Heavenly Father,

I'm overwhelmed by Your goodness. All these people coming together to celebrate with us today brings me so much joy! I trust that whoever is meant to be here with us will be here. You have placed so many incredible people in our lives that I can't imagine my wedding day without them. It is a tremendous blessing to have my family and friends here to share, celebrate, and witness what You have done! Lord, I pray that a witness is exactly what our wedding will be—a witness to who You are and all that You have done!

I know it doesn't seem like it, but this day is not about us. It's about You. It's about Your love and Your redemption. It's Your story, unfolding right before our very eyes—a beautiful and amazing story that we get to participate in. Thank You, Father! We are Your ambassadors, Your workmanship. Thank You for choosing us to represent You through marriage. Thank You for entrusting us with this sacred gift. Help us to be faithful to what You have called us to do today, knowing that You have fully prepared us in every way.

Lord, I pray that other couples would be encouraged today. That they would be motivated to love deeply and pursue You because they've witnessed our love for You and each other. I pray that love that has died would be resurrected! That broken marriages would be healed and made whole. For our friends and family members who are not married, I pray that they would witness today what it looks like to be equally yoked in marriage. Lord, You can do this—in fact, You can do immeasurably more than all we could ever ask or imagine (Ephesians 3:20).

My greatest desire for our wedding day is that our guests would see You, Lord; that Your presence would be undeniable because of the way _____ and I love each other. When people witness our love in action, move them to want to know You. May You be so evident in every detail of this day that people are drawn to You.

When our wedding celebration is all said and done, I pray that because of Your love and presence, no one would forget this day. Lord, I pray that as much as my husband and I radiate You today, that we would continue to abide in You and radiate Your glory for the rest of our lives.

In Jesus's name, amen.

. . . .

My God will meet all your needs according to the riches of his glory in Christ Jesus.
PHILIPPIANS 4:19

You may ask me for anything in my name, and I will do it.
JOHN 14:14

No one should seek their own good, but the good of others.
1 CORINTHIANS 10:24

FROM THIS DAY FORWARD

Lord,

It's our wedding day! It's finally here, and yet it will go by so fast. It's one day, and yet a lifetime follows.

That's really what our wedding day represents—the rest of our lives.

Lord, thank You for life here on earth and the promise and reality of forever. Thank You that _____ and I get to spend the rest of our lives together, loving each other the way You love us. Lord, I pray that the love, joy, and passion we have on our wedding day would lead only to more of the same for the rest of our lives. I pray that our love would grow as we fall more in love with You. That we would not stop pursuing each other and pursuing You. I pray that we would continue to become more like Jesus from our wedding day forward. That we would trust in the good work You have started in us to mold and shape our marriage so that it reflects Your love.

This day is so significant and means so much to us . . . yet I believe You have greater things in store, things that are immeasurably more than all we can ever ask or imagine. Thank You for the everlasting covenant that _____ and I will make today. Help us remember the vows we speak and the promises we make. Help us diligently guard and protect them as we daily seek You. May the vows we make today always represent the sacred covenant You have created.

From this day forward, may we never forget what You have done.

From this day forward, help us to put each other before ourselves.

From this day forward, help us to love You more than anything or anyone.

From this day forward, may our love be a beacon of hope for people searching for true, unconditional love.

From this day forward, let Your love define who we are.

From this day forward, may our marriage be greater than we ever could have imagined.

From this day forward, what You have brought together, let no one separate.

From this day forward, let our love be fearless, sacrificial, and selfless.

Thank You for all that You have in store for our lives. Our wedding day is only the beginning of a love story that points to Your love story. Thank You!

In Jesus's name, amen.

. . . .

Commit to the LORD whatever you do,
and he will establish your plans.
PROVERBS 16:3

He has made everything beautiful in its time.
He has also set eternity in the human heart; yet no one can fathom
what God has done from beginning to end.
ECCLESIASTES 3:11

And now these three remain: faith, hope and love.
But the greatest of these is love.
1 CORINTHIANS 13:13

The Mother
of the
Bride

Congratulations!

Your daughter is getting married! As soon as my firsborn, Erin, got engaged, we were swept up in the wedding planning whirlwind. We were crazy excited and could not help but move full steam ahead. While this is not a bad thing, it's definitely not God's best. I know, because thankfully, He graciously slammed on the planning brakes when Erin had her first meltdown. I knew it was coming, and while I am now grateful for the frustration and fear that caused Erin's tears, it was still hard. By God's grace, however, it became a beautiful mess that brought forth precious gifts from God as well as the message and purpose of this book.

Prayer.

More than anything, what you and I need to do as mothers of the bride is pray. Not just occasionally, when it's convenient, or when there's a bride meltdown, or as a last resort, but every single day, throughout the day. Because the truth is, prayer matters more than the perfect wedding dress . . . more than the first dance song . . . more than the flowers; it matters more than the venue, the food, the reception, the entertainment, or the color of the bridesmaids' dresses. Even more than the vows they speak and the rings they exchange—prayer matters more than anything.

Let me say it again—as you plan and prepare, prayer will be more important than anything and everything else you do.

It will prepare your daughter to become the bride and wife that God created her to be. It will be the driving force behind every decision, from the most important to the most minor. It will be a critical part of the firm foundation upon which God will build and strengthen your daughter and her soon-to-be husband's relationship and life together. And to be frank, prayer will be the key to survival—hers and yours. It seems like just yesterday that I cradled my daughter in my arms. How swiftly the years go by. Three-hundred-fifty-four days from right now, she'll be getting married. I don't know how you're handling all this with your daughter, but I'm a mess—a good mess, though. It's a once-in-a-lifetime kind of beautiful mess. I am all over the place in my heart and head . . .

- overthinking and analyzing
- praying (constantly)
- overwhelmed with joy and gratitude
- crying—a lot
- reminiscing. And, yes, looking through photo albums of her when she was little
- acting crazy and calm and excited . . . and sometimes noticeably anxious
- maybe letting my control-freak, hurricane-mom side get the best of me more than I would like to admit
- having so much to do and not knowing what to do first all at the same time

Please tell me you can relate! We are not the first moms to go through this, and we will not be the last. That being said, how's your wedding planning going? Did you buy a mother-of-the-bride guide yet? Here's where we are in our planning efforts so far:

- Erin and Parker have set their date.
- Our invite list is still a work in progress.
- We have selected the wedding ceremony venue.
- We have talked to our pastor about the ceremony and premarital counseling, so that is all in the works.
- We have looked at a few places for the reception, but because of the number of guests, we are limited, so we are not sure where the reception will be at this point.
- *Save the Dates* are ordered.
- Erin has selected her maid of honor.
- Erin knows who she will ask to be her bridesmaids, but she hasn't asked yet.
- We are in the process of deciding how to ask the wedding party, hoping to come up with something unique and creative.
- We are discussing the idea of hiring a professional wedding planner.
- We have decided who will sing at the wedding ceremony.

While there are still so many unknowns at this point, there is one thing I *do* know. God is still God! He is sovereign and doesn't have to run to Brooks Brothers to score a new suit for the reception while we plan the wedding. No matter what lies ahead, He is faithful, loving, gracious, and good; I can trust Him completely with everything. And so can you.

Ahh, I feel so much better, don't you? Because let's be honest, there are a ton of things we don't know as we journey through life. So many *what ifs* to be fearful of and fret over, so many bad things that could happen, and so much to do right that could go wrong! And yet, despite life's unknowns and uncertainties, we have a good, caring Father in heaven. A Savior who has made Himself known, so that when we fear the unknown, we can trust the One who knows.

Resting in this reality, we can rely on the foundational truths He has given us through His Word, the Bible. This is good news! It changes everything, including how you and I approach and appreciate our daughters' weddings and every minute of every day in preparation for that day. We may not know what tomorrow holds, but we know who holds tomorrow.

Friend, your daughter is getting married. Life as you know it is going to change drastically. So let's pray—we'll do it together. I have already prayed the prayers written in this book for Erin and her fiancé. The Bible verses shared at the end of each prayer topic hold solid, life-changing truths from God's Word that I highly encourage you to read out loud. You might also consider writing these passages on 3x5 cards and making an effort to memorize them, hide them in your heart, and let them guide you as this beautiful drama unfolds. That's what my approach has been, and it has made my prayer life that much brighter, my load that much lighter, and all that's right that much "righter." God's Word has blessed me immeasurably in my walk with Him. Lastly, the wedding tips scattered throughout this book are lessons that Erin and I learned along the way that we believe might help you and your daughter.

This is such an exciting time!

Let's get started . . .

Heavenly Father,

Thank You for the gift of love. We can have it all in this life—fame, fortune, power, respect, admiration, friendship, family, joy, laughter—in fact, we can have everything the world offers and all the heart craves, yet, without love, we have nothing. Without You, we have nothing. Apart from You and Your love, life is vacant and our souls are void of purpose and meaning. Lord, You *are* love. Without You, love does not exist. Therefore, we cannot experience true, trustworthy, authentic love apart from You.

Heavenly Father, anything that is worth a lot, costs a lot; and Your love for us cost You everything—Your Son's very life. You loved us so much that You gave us Jesus, the greatest gift, the greatest sacrifice, Your one and only Son. Your love is sacrificial. Your love continuously gives. Through You, we see that love is a sacrifice; a continual giving of one's self without any strings attached, without expectations or reciprocation.

The world and the culture we live in try to redefine love in ways that are contrary to what You created it to be. If the world's selfish kind of love (which is not love at all) has jaded my daughter and her fiancé's understanding of love in any way, please, Lord, help them to see through the lies and fully embrace Your truth.

God, don't let the spirit of the world or the lust of the flesh seep into their understanding and dilute the reality of Your perfect, unconditional love. _____ and _____ cannot know or experience love unless Your love abides in them and prevails over all else. Please, God, never let either of them be content with just knowing *about* Your love. Instead, grant them a hunger, thirst, and passion to intimately know Your love in all its fullness. They cannot love You, themselves, each other, or others unless they have received the love that You have for them.

Today I pray that my daughter and her fiancé's hearts and minds would be filled to overflowing with a greater understanding of the breadth and depth of Your boundless love. To the greatest extent possible this side of eternity, bless them with an unrivaled intimacy with You that results in them experiencing love in such a profound way that they will never be the same.

Father, I pray that Your immeasurable, all-consuming love would define who my daughter and her fiancé are so that they will never search for love or satisfaction anywhere else. Because this young couple's hearts are filled to overflowing with *Your* love, I pray that *their* love would abound more and more in knowledge and depth of insight. Let Your everlasting love pour forth from their lives, so that every life they touch is changed and drawn to You.

Lord, I pray that from this moment on, You will be _____ and _____'s first love. When other "loves" try to entice them away from You, please draw them back to Your heart where there is protection and safety. Please help them to delight in You so that the desires of their hearts can be fulfilled. I pray that they will love each other unconditionally, sacrificially, and wholeheartedly.

Father, I pray that my daughter and her fiancé's love for each other would mirror Yours. As they prepare for their wedding, please, God, prepare their hearts one day at a time to know and love You more, so they would then love one another as completely and perfectly as a man and woman can.

In Jesus's name, amen.

. . . .

We love because he first loved us.

1 JOHN 4:19

Dear Lord,

"What is the purpose of life?" "Why am I here?" Most people spend their entire lives searching for the answers to these questions that resonate from the depths of the human heart. From relationships to work, from accolades to power, from prosperity to fame—with great desperation, they seek purpose and meaning in the fading treasures of this world.

Even King Solomon, the wisest and wealthiest man of his day, pondered the meaning of life. He had it all; but that wasn't enough. Your Word tells us that Solomon possessed everything the world had to offer, and yet he discovered it was all meaningless. "I denied myself nothing my eyes desired; I refused my heart no pleasure. My heart took delight in all my labor, and this was the reward for all my toil. Yet when I surveyed all that my hands had done and what I had toiled to achieve, everything was meaningless, a chasing after the wind; nothing was gained under the sun" (Ecclesiastes 2:10–11).

Heavenly Father, what Solomon eventually discovered is what people desperately need to know today: that apart from You, life has no purpose or meaning. Lord, _____ and _____ will never understand the meaning of life and marriage unless they know You. Please help them to truly know You, Lord, not just know about You. Help them to see the world and each other through Your eyes. As they grow in their love and knowledge of You, please help them live according to Your purpose.

Jesus, You are the purpose of life and marriage. In Christ, _____ and _____ are loved, chosen, forgiven, redeemed, sanctified, and set free. In Christ, they are called to be the salt of the earth and light of the world (Matthew 5:13–16). Father, please help them know who they are in Christ.

Help them to love You more than themselves, more than comfort and convenience, more than the pursuit of dreams and desires, more than anything in this world. When temptations arise that would compromise who they are in Christ, please bless them with hearts fully committed to You, so that they would never choose to waver, give in, or give up.

To know Your will and purpose, we must spend time in Your Word. Lord, please help _____ and _____ hold to Your teachings and continue in Your Word so they can know the truth and be set free to live according to Your divine purpose. This world offers so many distractions that could keep them from obeying You and what You have called them to do. Lord, please bless them with wisdom and discernment so that instead of being led astray, they are fully prepared to do Your will, no matter what.

Both life and marriage are expressions of the same purpose—to know, love, and glorify You. And although love is among the greatest blessings in marriage, it is not the sole purpose. Lord Jesus, You want _____ and _____ to be holy, as You are holy. Their marriage is not a path to happiness, but to holiness. Father, please help them to live by the power of the Holy Spirit and not according to the world. Please teach them how to remain completely set apart for You in a culture that tries to integrate them into a worldly existence. Their wedding day will be an incredible opportunity to display Your love and holiness. As they prepare and plan for the most important day of their lives, please help them to trust You and live for You, one day at a time. Heavenly Father, please help them to fix their eyes on Jesus, the very purpose of life and marriage.

In Jesus's precious name I pray, amen.

. . . .

We know that in all things God works for the good of those who love him,
who have been called according to his purpose.

ROMANS 8:28

Father,

Prayer is the purpose and goal of this book. We want to draw near to You, to spend time with You, to talk with and listen to You. We want to be still in Your presence.

You know all things. You know the words we will speak before they are spoken. You know the motivations and deepest desires of our hearts. You know us more intimately than we could ever know ourselves. You always know what we need—even before we come to You in prayer, You are already at work in our daily lives orchestrating every complex detail in response to the cry of our hearts. At all times and in every circumstance, You know what's best for us and are committed to us, regardless of what it may cost.

Lord, please help my daughter and her fiancé, as individuals and as a couple, to diligently and wholeheartedly seek You. I pray that prayer would not be just a response to the needs they have, but a way of life. May all the threads in the tapestry of their lives be woven together with prayer. In fact, I pray that they would be an example to all who know them of what it looks like to pray without ceasing. In addition to coming to You for their needs and concerns, please teach them to hide Your Word in their hearts, so they know the truth, and therefore walk in freedom and pray accordingly.

Lord, help them understand and appreciate the sacrifice Jesus made on their behalf to make prayer possible. Help them not take that for granted. May they have an enduring and deep understanding of the priceless privilege it is to come boldly before the throne of grace. Teach _____ and _____ to pray as You taught Your earliest followers; protect them from a trite, meaningless, repetitive, shallow, shopping-list prayer life.

Help them see prayer as the powerful weapon it is and to understand why it is vital to their relationship with You and each other. Lord, help them to learn and grow into a lifestyle of prayer, where they choose to pray about everything, from their most inconsequential decisions to the life-changing choices they will face. In every circumstance, at all times, I pray that prayer would be their immediate and first response.

Lord, You don't always give us exactly what we pray for. You see the puzzle pieces of our lives and how they fit perfectly together. You answer our prayers according to Your perfect will and plan. We might not always understand Your ways or how You choose to respond to our pleas, but we can always trust Your heart. Lord, when my daughter and her fiancé's prayers do not bring the answer or outcome they hope for, please comfort them. Please wrap them in Your peace that surpasses all understanding. Guard their hearts and minds from fear, pride, bitterness, or anything else that would cause them to doubt Your goodness and love for them. Help them learn to trust that Your plans for their lives are determined by Your desire for their highest good.

Father, bless _____ and _____ with hearts that overflow with Your Spirit, hearts that long for Your will to be done above and beyond their own. Give them broken and contrite hearts that beat to deny themselves and follow You. Let their hearts overflow with just as much godly peace when the answer to their petition is "no" as it is when the answer is "yes." I ask for hearts that are teeming with a love for You and for each other that is so all-encompassing that prayer is something they *live* even more than something they *do*.

In Jesus's name, amen.

. . . .

Devote yourselves to prayer, being watchful and thankful.
COLOSSIANS 4:2

TRUTH AND
THE WORD OF GOD

Heavenly Father,

You gave us the Word of God so we could come to know and love You—the God of the Word. The Bible is the greatest love story ever told. It reveals all we need to know about You and the awesome plans You have for creation. Your Word is dependable and trustworthy. It's alive and active, drawing us ever closer to You, Lord.

Your Word is timeless. It is just as applicable to our lives today as it was when it was originally written. You divinely inspired every word; nothing has been forgotten or left out. Therefore, we have everything we need to live according to Your perfect plan for our lives. Thank You!

Lord, I pray that _____ and _____ would love Your Word and look forward to and appreciate spending time with You. I pray that they will make reading the Bible a top priority together, no matter what is going on in their lives or how busy they get. Father, let Your Word be the strong foundation upon which they build their lives. When they have decisions to make or when questions arise pertaining to how You want them to live, I pray they would immediately seek direction and guidance from Your Word. Please help them not take the Bible for granted or regard it casually.

Scripture searches the hearts, thoughts, and attitudes of those who seek You, Father. I pray that _____ and _____ would not only seek You, but learn to study and properly handle Your Word. Second Timothy 2:15 admonishes us, "Do your best to present yourself to God as one approved, a worker who does not need to be ashamed and who correctly handles the word of truth." Lord, please help them wield the "sword of the Spirit, which is the word of God" (Ephesians 6:17) effectively, driving forces of darkness back from their lives.

Dear God, as _____ and _____ study and use the Word of God, may they be careful to share the whole counsel of the Bible and not distort or compromise the truth or tell others what they want to hear. Instead, give them the grace and love to accurately present the Word of God in its fullness whenever the opportunity presents itself.

Father, please remind _____ and _____ that Your Word never returns void or unfulfilled, but always accomplishes what You intend it to do, just as Isaiah 55:11 declares: "So is my word that goes out from my mouth: It will not return to me empty, but will accomplish what I desire and achieve the purpose for which I sent it."

God, I ask that You would hide Your Word in their hearts that they might not sin against You (Psalm 119:11). As they continue to read Scripture each day, please mold and shape their hearts and lives into the image of Your Son, Jesus. And as they learn and grow in wisdom and knowledge, I pray they would boldly proclaim Your Word as they should.

Throughout the entire wedding weekend, Father, I pray that Your Word would be spoken with power. When Scripture is read during the wedding ceremony, open people's hearts and minds to hear and receive the truth. During the wedding ceremony and reception, I pray that You would be exalted and that our guests would be blessed by Your powerful, life-changing presence. Lord, I pray that You are magnified in and through every aspect of _____ and _____'s wedding celebration.

In Jesus's name, amen.

. . . .

I have hidden your word in my heart that I might not sin against you.

PSALM 119:11

Challenge #1

As a mother, you share a unique love and perspective with God toward your daughter. A love only a mother can fully appreciate and understand. Jesus used the word *Father* to describe God because that is who God is and how He relates to us. As a mother, your unique, loving vantage point enables you to understand His heart like only a mother can. For mother-of-the-bride Challenge #1, I would like for you to consider writing your daughter a letter filled with words of love, hope, and encouragement. Tell her about your wedding experience; how you felt when you put your wedding dress on for the first time or what it was like the night before your wedding day—how did you feel and what did you pray? Maybe consider telling your daughter what you imagine God might be thinking about her as she prepares her heart to enter into the beautiful covenant of marriage.

Before you start writing, pray. Ask God to give you wisdom and words so you can openly and honestly share your heart. After you're done writing the letter, place it in an envelope and, again, pray! Pray that when your daughter reads the letter, she will be blessed and encouraged. You can give her the letter whenever you feel led to do so, or you can save it for when she's having a bridezilla kind of a day.

*I*t seems so obvious, doesn't it? This book is filled with prayer and your daughter is getting married, so of course you're praying. Well, friend, hear me out. And trust me when I tell you that I need this as much as you do. You can never pray too much, and yet, there will be moments when you get so caught up in everything else . . . that you'll forget to pray. Yes, I said it. You will forget. The world won't blow up, and the wedding will still be amazing—but there will be moments when prayer and praise should be your first response instead of your last resort.

I don't want you to forget. I don't want you to miss out on the countless opportunities you will have to stop in the midst of everything so that you can pray and *thank God*. And not only thank Him, but praise Him. Praise Him for who He is and all that He has done and all that He will do. Thank Him for every moment, no matter how perfect or horrible, because every moment is a gift from God. Every moment is an opportunity to look at life through the lens of His love and grace.

Your daughter is getting married. It's amazing! But you know what's more amazing? Jesus. He loves you perfectly and unconditionally. He has blessed you and your family beyond measure, in ways too numerous to count. He has given you meaning and purpose, and He's provided you with everything you need for life and godliness. He started a good work in you and will be faithful to complete it. He holds your life in His mighty hands and rejoices over you with singing. (Wait a minute—can you even imagine what it sounds like to hear the Lord sing?) He forgives and forgets. He redeems, restores, and resurrects. He, saves, sets free, and sanctifies. He heals and makes holy. *Wow!* He is worthy to be praised!

Remember, your daughter and your future son-in-law are His. Their wedding, all the planning and preparation leading up to the big day, the ceremony and reception—every single detail regarding their lives as a married couple—all His. He is the One holding it all together. Including your sanity. He's the One working all things together for His glory and your good. He is God, and He is blessing you with a once-in-a-lifetime event—your daughter's wedding. I cannot tell you how many times I needed to remind myself of this during the twelve months we had to prepare for Erin's wedding. And every time I took the time to pray and praise the Lord, everything changed, even when the circumstances didn't.

So what's my first tip? Pray about everything and praise Him for everything, because this wedding is a once-in-a-lifetime event. You will never get these moments back. And you will never regret taking the time to *pray* and *praise God!*

Father,

I am so grateful that You are trustworthy. I can trust You completely, no matter what. All relationships are built on love and trust. We may love someone, but we cannot feel safe and secure in a love relationship if we don't have trust. I continue to pray for _____ and _____ as they prepare for their wedding; my prayer is that they would trust You and each other implicitly.

Help them to take the risks necessary to trust each other in every area of their relationship. Help them to be intentional and vulnerable—with hearts wide open! Lord, encourage them to move forward and persevere in order to learn to trust each other more and more. Give them the grace to sincerely and honestly communicate, to show compassion, and to truly understand one another. Don't let the sun go down on their anger, Lord; help them be quick to hear, slow to speak, and slow to get angry (James 1:19). Give them the grace to be forgiving when the other is hurtful or careless with their words. Bless them with an extraordinary commitment to their love that will allow them to trust each other and resolve conflicts when they arise.

Father, I pray that _____ and _____ would see that trust is built in stages and is not a finished product. Help them realize that challenges like disappointment, hurt, and frustration are often the very tools You use to strengthen and cultivate trust in a love relationship. Grow their trust in You, Lord.

Help them understand that trust matures through trials and challenges, especially when it is not easy to trust You. Grant them the courage to persevere when conditions tempt them to harden their hearts. Open their eyes to the reality that their trust in You is in no way contingent on the events unfolding in their lives.

Father, I pray that You give _____ and _____ hearts that delight in You above all else. Hearts that long to trust You more as they journey through life together. Lord, in many ways, the question is not how deeply we trust You, but how deeply You can trust us! And I want that for them, Lord. I pray that their individual relationships with You would be pure and true. That they each would be faithful with little, so that You might entrust them with much.

Lord, please help _____ and _____ trust You and lean not on their own understanding. Teach them to acknowledge You in all their ways and be vigilant to guard their hearts that they each might be wholly surrendered and dedicated to You.

And when they blow it, Lord, and let You down like we all do, grant them the grace to humbly come to You, own up, and repent. Don't let pride, frustration, anger, or any other sin separate them from You. Instead, may they trust You and fall into Your everlasting love and be restored.

In Jesus's name, amen.

. . . .

Blessed is the one who trusts in the LORD, whose confidence is in him.
They will be like a tree planted by the water that sends out its roots
by the stream. It does not fear when heat comes; its leaves are always green.
It has no worries in a year of drought and never fails to bear fruit.

JEREMIAH 17:7–8

FORGIVENESS

Dear God,

In seeking to walk in Your forgiveness, we cannot know, experience, or extend forgiveness if we have not first received it from You. In addition, we will not seek forgiveness if we do not first understand why we need to be forgiven. When we come to understand our desperate need, it leads us to repentance and then to forgiveness.

Lord, first and foremost, I pray that You would help _____ and _____ understand how much they have been forgiven. Please help them comprehend the depth of their need and, thus, the endless supply of grace, mercy, and forgiveness You extend to them, no matter what.

There will be many opportunities for _____ and _____ to forgive each other; that's life and marriage. Lord, I pray they would be quick to forgive and never let the sun go down while they are still angry. Keep them from harboring resentment or holding grudges against each other or anyone else. Withholding forgiveness ends up hurting the person who needs to forgive more than the one who needs to be forgiven. No matter what the offense or deep hurt that has been experienced, unforgiveness must never be an option. It is never good, and it is never Your will.

Please help them to know that extending forgiveness does not say that what happened or the hurt it caused is okay; nor does it justify the evil that has been done. What happened is still wrong. It still hurts. And it is still unacceptable. But let them know that forgiveness frees them from carrying the weight of the burden that only Jesus was meant to bear.

Lord, help my daughter and her fiancé to know that they do not need to take matters into their own hands—that You will fight for them, just as You have promised. Vengeance is and always will be Yours. But even so, Lord, when they need to extend forgiveness, whether it be to each other or someone else, I pray that they would do more than forgive. Help them to forgive and pray for the one who hurt them. Let them relate to that person with all the godliness, love, and redemptive beauty that Jesus would.

You instruct us in Your Word to pray for our enemies. Well, this, as You know, is difficult to do. But it's not optional. It's not a choice. The circumstances and measure of pain do not grant us the privilege of choosing whether to obey Your commands. No, Your Word clearly instructs us to forgive and to pray, to treat others the way we want to be treated. And that's exactly what I pray this couple will do—obey and do what Your Word says. Not because they feel like it or want to, but because they love You and would rather obey You than take an easier path and go their own way.

Father, You are faithful and trustworthy. If You tell us to do something, no matter how difficult or crazy it might seem to us, it is always for our good and Your glory. Thank You, Lord.

In Jesus's name, amen.

. . . .

Blessed is the one whose transgressions are forgiven, whose sins are covered.
Blessed is the one whose sin the Lord does not count
against them and in whose spirit is no deceit.

PSALM 32:1-2

Heavenly Father,

My daughter is getting married! We have so much to be thankful for and so many reasons to worship and praise You. You are amazing! There is no end to Your outrageous love and goodness. And while one blessing follows another, the source is always You—Your character and generous heart. Thank You for all that You have done in _____ and _____'s lives thus far. Thank You for the good work You started that brought them together for such a time as this. It's a good work that You have also promised to faithfully complete. What a blessing! This wedding and their future life together are beautiful demonstrations of Your love and faithfulness. You are so good. Thank You, Father!

Lord, You know what is best for my daughter and her soon-to-be husband. You know everything about them, including the deep desires of their hearts. We live in a broken, sin-drenched world, so our desires tend to be selfish, jaded, and worldly. But Your Word says that if we delight in You, You will give us the desires of our hearts (Psalm 37:4). So, Lord, I pray that _____ and _____ would desire You more than anything else. I pray that they would sincerely and wholeheartedly delight in You, and as a result, that their desires would be in sync with Your purposes.

Lord, I pray that they would have hearts that are deeply thankful for who You are and all that You have done. Gratitude is an attitude of the heart. Please search their hearts and reveal any offensive attitude, pride, or arrogance in their lives. Dear God, I pray that they would not take You for granted, either individually or together as husband and wife. Please keep their relationship with You pure and undiluted with compromise or mediocrity. Instead,

Lord, I pray that they will enter Your gates with thanksgiving in their hearts and Your courts with praise.

Lord, bless my daughter and future son-in-law with an abiding gratitude for each other. Help them see one another as You see them—as deeply loved, chosen, and treasured. Heavenly Father, I pray that they would be filled with thankfulness for Your unfailing love; that they would see their marriage as one of Your greatest blessings.

As life happens with its challenges, trials, and tests, I pray that _____ and _____ would claim Scripture as the solid foundation for their lives. May they desire to spend as much time as possible reading Your Word and spending time with You. Help them to be grateful for Your unfailing love and cling to the hope they have in Your promises, both in the best of times and the worst of times. When circumstances in life weigh heavy, please allow what You have promised to strengthen their attitude of gratitude. Please help _____ and _____ see the value in their trials, the treasure that they have in each other, and above all, the surpassing significance of a thankful heart that loves You more than anything else.

In Jesus's mighty name, amen.

. . . .

Always giving thanks to God the Father for everything,
in the name of our Lord Jesus Christ.
EPHESIANS 5:20

WISDOM

Father God,

It seems that in many ways, life is a string of choices and decisions, each somehow connected and leading to the next. Oftentimes, we end up making decisions apart from Your guidance with no regard to the consequences or outcome. Why do we do this? Why do we choose to go our own way? Lord, we need You. We need guidance and insight. We need wisdom.

Father, please help _____ and _____ purposefully and passionately pursue wisdom from above—Your wisdom. Wisdom that is more precious than rubies or gold or any other earthly treasure. Help them pursue wisdom so that their decisions bring You glory and draw them closer to Your heart. May they both understand and walk in the fear of the Lord, for the Bible declares that this is the beginning of wisdom.

I pray also that this young couple would understand the difference between the world's wisdom and heaven's wisdom. James 3:15–16 tells us that this world's wisdom is earthly and unspiritual, cultivating "envy and selfish ambition . . . disorder and every evil practice." James 3:17 shows us that the wisdom coming from heaven is "pure . . . peace-loving, considerate, submissive, full of mercy and good fruit, impartial, and sincere." Father, help them walk in Your heavenly wisdom and readily recognize its earthly counterfeit.

Heavenly Father, You tell us You will give us wisdom generously if we ask for it. Please, encourage _____ and _____ to come boldly before Your throne to ask for wisdom in every situation, especially as it pertains to issues in their marriage. When they do seek You for wisdom, Lord, I pray that they would trust You to honor Your Word and give it to them. Possessing wisdom is essential, but putting it into action in our everyday lives is vital to living an abundant, God-honoring life. Father, motivate _____ and _____ to apply Your wisdom to every decision they make—from the most minute to the most monumental.

The world, the flesh, and the devil can throw deadly distractions at us. Please keep this couple alert to the schemes of darkness and equip them with everything they need for the battles they will face. Help them to know You and Your Word intimately. Help them follow You with passion as they walk with Christ, for in You are hidden all the treasures of wisdom and knowledge.

Finally, Lord, teach both my daughter and my son-in-law to number their days so that they can gain a heart of wisdom just as Psalm 90:12 promises. Let them walk with eternity in view, realizing that neither the next breath nor the next heartbeat is promised to anyone.

In Jesus's name, amen.

. . . .

Do not forsake wisdom, and she will protect you;
love her, and she will watch over you.
The beginning of wisdom is this: Get wisdom.
Though it cost all you have, get understanding.
PROVERBS 4:6-7

Lord,

You are the author of relationships—You created us to be in loving relationships with You and other people. Communication is vital in relationships. It is impossible to know, love, trust, or obey You if we are not in constant communion with You. Thank You for the gift of faith that makes it possible for us to freely and confidently draw near to You. Not a moment goes by that we don't need You! Thank You for always being ready and willing to listen and respond to our cries for help.

Father, although You have given us many forms of communication, the most common is the spoken word. Lord, please help _____ and _____ to use their words wisely with the utmost care and caution. Search their hearts each day and let the words from their mouths and the meditations of their hearts be pleasing in Your sight (Psalm 19:14). I ask You to fill _____ and _____ with truth, so that from the overflow of their hearts, their words will reflect Your love and life. Help them speak words of encouragement and edification in order to strengthen and build each other up.

Father, convict _____ and _____ when they speak harshly, insensitively, or negatively to each other. When the words they speak cause harm to each other, help them make every effort to forgive, reconcile, and restore communication. Please enable _____ and _____ to communicate clearly and confidently without confusion. Lord, fill their hearts with gratitude, so that rather than complaining or arguing, they will speak words of thanksgiving and joy.

Lord, making and keeping promises is vital to building trust in a relationship. Without trust, authentic communication is impossible. God, before _____ and _____ can make and keep promises and build trust in their relationship, they must first trust You. You are the foundation and the example. Lord, please help them trust You more as they spend time with You in Your Word and prayer. Another vital aspect of healthy communication is listening. Lord, help _____ and _____ to be good listeners. Give them open ears and humble hearts that long to listen, understand, and appreciate what is shared in conversation. As they listen, help _____ and _____ sincerely care and be genuinely interested in what they have to say to each other. Eliminate the distractions that vie for their attention so they can take the time to focus, listen, and communicate.

When it comes to planning a wedding, communication is key. There are so many important and timely decisions that must be made. Father, You already know how this is all going to turn out. You know exactly what _____ and _____ need to discuss right now to make unified decisions that reflect Your will. Father, please reveal Yourself and meet them right where they are in this moment. Bless them with Your presence and peace. Please give them wisdom and guidance. Help them to be still and listen to Your voice. Lord, in the midst of all the wedding planning excitement and chaos, help them focus on You and the reason they're getting married.

More than anything, I pray Your amazing love and grace will be communicated in and through _____ and _____ throughout their entire wedding day. Lord, when _____ and _____ speak to each other and their guests, please allow Your Word to go forth with power. May their actions speak louder than their words and be a reflection of Your love.

In Jesus's name, amen.

• •

Words kill, words give life; they're either poison or fruit—you choose.
PROVERBS 18:21 MSG

Challenge #2

My friend and fellow mother of the bride, you're not done writing letters. This one is going to be similar to the first. However, instead of writing to your daughter, you're going to write a thank-you letter to your future son-in-law. Tell him how grateful you are for him and why. Be as specific as possible as you elaborate on the goodness of God in making him a part of your family. Again, pray before you start writing and ask God to help you share your heart with the man your daughter plans to spend the rest of her life with.

Okay, maybe you're trying to juggle a hectic mother-of-the-bride schedule right now. I get it. If you don't have time to sit down and write a letter, at the very least, send the young man a card. You, your daughter, and your future son-in-law will be blessed as a result.

Confession time: *Shhh*, don't tell anyone . . . I'm a recovering control freak. What does that mean? Well, although I'm better today than I was yesterday, I have a tendency to think that I know what's best for my daughters. And because I think I know what's best, I'm always willing to share my opinion and guidance—when the girls ask for it and when they don't.

The great news is that I am a work in progress to the glory of God, and so are my daughters. And so are you.

Part of the good work God is doing in my life is that He is graciously helping me to know and trust that *He* is always in control, over everything. While this truth seems obvious, sometimes I live as though it's not. And I'm sure I'm not the only one who does this. I think it's safe to say we could all use a refresher course in letting go, letting God, and learning to trust Him more every day. For moms like me, this is a one-day-at-a-time, one-prayer-at-a-time journey.

Ultimately, your daughter's wedding is your daughter's wedding—not yours! Erin's wedding is not my wedding—it's hers. If you have lost sight of this along the way, allow me to graciously encourage you to stop trying to manipulate and control your daughter's amazing, once-in-a-lifetime wedding. Stop thinking that you know what's best because she's your daughter and you know her better than anyone on the planet.

Instead . . . breathe! And pray!

Please, learn from what I have walked through, my friend, and let your daughter take the lead. In every decision from this day forward, let her do what she feels led to do. If she's not open to your suggestions, pray that she would be. If she asks for your opinion, share with enthusiasm but allow her to take ownership. *Feel free to make suggestions, but don't overdo it.* When she invites you in, be available and get involved in every aspect of the planning. As hard as it is, do not be offended or angry if she decides to do the exact opposite of what you would do or what you suggested. It's okay. *It is okay*; it really is. Just . . . pray. And then pray some more. God wants your relationship with your daughter to grow and deepen during this season of wedding planning. Don't you want the same?

CALLING

Father,

Thank You for creating us on purpose for a purpose. What a blessing and privilege it is to know, love, and be called by You. Lord, there is no safer place than in the center of Your will. And so I ask with all my heart that _____ and _____ would bravely pursue Your call, knowing that Your plans for them are always good. And if that call leads them beyond their comfort zones, I pray that they would have the courage, faith, and strength to move onward and upward in pursuit of Your call on their lives.

God, they cannot pursue a call they are unaware or unsure of. Please give them wisdom and clarity—let them hear and know Your voice above the clamor and chaos of the many voices that vie for their attention. Bless them with the faith to stay committed to You and Your call. Help them to stay humble and fully open to Your leading, to any change of direction, and especially to Your call to wait—for that is often the hardest. Lord, when they are unsure of where You want them to go or what You want them to do, please give them the patience necessary to wait on You and pray until Your Spirit moves them to action.

Father, there will be times when they blow it; we all do that. Please help them remember that no matter how bad the mess, You are gracious, kind, and patient. You will redeem their mistakes. Give them grace and forgiveness so that whoever stumbles may be helped back up by the other, forgiven, and encouraged to shake it off and continue the race.

Let them never forget that they have been called for a purpose, as stated in Romans 8:28. Father, Your purpose is that they become increasingly more like Your Son. Help them to recognize this reality and seek You as a married couple and individually. Help them fix their eyes on You, not on their own wants and desires. Lord, if they seek You, they will find exactly what You have for them.

May they remain ever faithful to You, living lives that are worthy of Your calling. I ask that they would love You wholeheartedly and keep Your commandments as they walk in the knowledge of Deuteronomy 7:9: "Know therefore that the LORD your God is God; he is the faithful God, keeping his covenant of love to a thousand generations of those who love him and keep his commandments."

Heavenly Father, You have a unique call and destiny for _____ and _____ that You have decreed they should fulfill together. I ask that You would fill them with a passionate love for You, each other, and their calling, so that Your glory shines through their individual lives and their marriage.

In Jesus's name, amen.

. . . .

I therefore, a prisoner for the Lord, urge you to walk in a manner
worthy of the calling to which you have been called, with all humility
and gentleness, with patience, bearing with one another in love,
eager to maintain the unity of the Spirit in the bond of peace.
EPHESIANS 4:1–3 ESV

Lord,

To best understand, comprehend, and pray about character—what it means and how it defines who we are and how we live—we must first look to You and Your character. We are fearfully and wonderfully made in Your image, so in order to know who we have been created to be, we must first look to our Creator. Heavenly Father, You have revealed Yourself through creation, Your Word, and Your Son, Jesus. You're not trying to hide from us. You want us to seek You and find You, because when we do, we find purpose, meaning, and everything else we need.

Lord, more than anything, as it pertains to my daughter and her fiancé, I pray that they would reflect Your character. Certainly, this is a lofty prayer because, unlike You, they are not perfect—they are each a work in progress. But the good news is that You're not finished with them. As they seek to know and love You more, You have faithfully promised to continue the good work You are doing in their lives. Because of that, as they grow into the image of Christ, their character will reflect Yours more each day as well.

When it comes to a person's character, there is so much to pray about. Character is who I am when no one is looking—the real me, deep down and unfiltered; it's the person You see and know intimately, Lord. Because You know _____ and _____ better than anyone, please give me wisdom and insight to pray for them according to Your will. Holy Spirit, please give me revelation regarding the character of God, so I can pray the way You would for my daughter and soon-to-be son-in-law.

Lord, help them walk in humility. Pride comes before destruction, bringing with it great evil, sin, chaos, deception, and confusion. Holy Spirit, if pride has taken root in either of their lives, I pray that You would make it known. Pierce their hearts with a conviction that leads to honest and sincere repentance, forgiveness, and full restoration. Lord, help _____ and _____ put each other's needs before their own. As they seek to honor You in every area of their lives, help them believe and rest in the reality that in Christ they are accepted, chosen, and set apart for Your glory.

Heavenly Father, I pray that my daughter and her fiancé's character, along with the quality of their marriage, would be defined by moral uprightness, integrity, decency, and honesty. Help them know what they believe and why. Give them courage to refuse to waver from living their convictions, no matter the cost. Inspire them to choose what is good, pure, admirable, and praiseworthy, so they become living examples for others to emulate. Lord, I also pray that their marriage would exemplify selflessness in a world characterized by self-centeredness. I pray that, despite differences in opinion, their oneness in Christ would create solidarity, helping them stand firm and undivided when it matters most.

When others observe _____ and _____, as individuals and as a married couple, whether it be during a season of blessing or heartbreak, I pray that those who see them would see Jesus.

In Jesus's precious name, I pray, amen.

. . . .

Whoever walks in integrity walks securely,
but whoever takes crooked paths will be found out.
PROVERBS 10:9

Lord,

We have so much to learn. Every moment of every day is filled with opportunities to deepen our knowledge and grow. To live *is* to learn. You created everything that exists, and in You, all things hold together. Everyone and everything finds its purpose and significance in and through You. Therefore, You are the ultimate source of all knowledge, wisdom, learning, and growing. We don't have to try to figure out how to live because, when we seek You, You direct our steps and guide us in the way we should go. When You created us, You started a good work and promised to complete it. Part of Your completion process is that we would learn how to live according to Your perfect will, plan, and purpose.

Father, _____ and _____ have so much to learn about You, about love, about each other, and about the world You created. It's impossible for either of them to get to the end of all there is to learn. Lord, bless them with humble, teachable, and willing spirits. Inspire them to dig deeper, ponder more, and listen longer. Many voices clamor for their attention and affection. Help them to hear and listen to Your voice first so they can grow in their relationship with You and each other.

_____ and _____ are a work in progress. Help them to respect where You have them in their walk with You as well as their relationship with each other. Marriage is fertile ground for learning and growing. Help them to be open and receptive to what You want to accomplish in and through them as individuals and as a couple. They are learning and growing in unique and different ways, but the goal is always the same: to become more like Jesus.

Sometimes in life we learn things that cause unhealthy habits or patterns. When these ungodly habits are confronted with the truth, they can be unlearned and replaced with healthy, godly habits. Lord, by the power of the Holy Spirit, I pray that You would renew _____ and _____'s minds with all that is true, holy, and good, so they can discern what is best and thereby replace old, unhealthy habits with new, life-giving ones.

Lord, although it comes with great benefits, growing involves change—and change often comes with pain. We tend to covet comfort. We like status quo living that involves as little change as possible. Change is hard. It includes making uncomfortable adjustments and sacrifices. As much as we try to avoid it, change is inevitable. But learning is not; we have a choice. We can resist change, or we can choose to learn and grow because of it.

Heavenly Father, please help _____ and _____ to *choose* to learn. Encourage them to be open and willing, no matter what changes they encounter during their lifetime together. When change is extremely difficult, even when loving becomes a challenge, dear Lord, I pray that they would take time to seek You first; that instead of reacting, they would pray and wait for direction so they can respond and move forward with wisdom and confidence.

Sometimes we must learn and grow through suffering. Lord, You know and understand this fully. Please give _____ and _____ submissive hearts that long to love You first and foremost through obedience to Your will. Father, I pray that they would be willing to suffer in order to obey You, resulting in a depth of knowledge and growth found no other way.

Furthermore, Lord, I pray that You will help them take what they learn and put it into practice. Let them walk it out in their marriage, in their individual lives, and within their spheres of influence. Help them support one another's calling and relationship with You in practical, loving ways that reflect

Your grace and kindness. I thank You that every day, they learn and grow, and as a result, You are being honored and glorified.

In Jesus's name, amen.

. . . .

This is what the LORD says—your Redeemer,
the Holy One of Israel: "I am the LORD your God,
who teaches you what is best for you,
who directs you in the way you should go."

ISAIAH 48:17

Teach me your way, LORD, and I may rely on your faithfulness;
give me an undivided heart, that I may fear your name.

PSALM 86:11

My sheep listen to my voice; I know them and they follow me.

JOHN 10:27

Dear Lord,

Everything we have is Yours. We came into this world with nothing, and that is exactly how we will depart. Even the air we breathe, that fills our lungs and provides us life, is a gift from You. When we understand that everything we have is Yours, we can be grateful no matter how much money or earthly treasure we have (or don't have). The truth is, we do not own anything. It is all Yours. And Father, You are so generous. Not only do You provide us with daily sustenance, You have graciously given us everything we need for life and godliness through Your precious Son, Jesus. He is the example of sincere and sacrificial giving. Through Him, we can choose to give generously and cheerfully.

God, giving isn't so much an issue of how much we part with as it is what's left after we give and why we give it. Really, it's a matter of the heart. Your Word describes an impoverished woman who, while she had very little to give, gave all she had. "As Jesus looked up, he saw the rich putting their gifts into the temple treasury. He also saw a poor widow put in two very small copper coins. 'Truly I tell you,' he said, 'this poor widow has put in more than all the others. All these people gave their gifts out of their wealth; but she out of her poverty put in all she had to live on'" (Luke 21:1–4).

What an outrageous and beautiful example of giving. Heavenly Father, that's how I hope my daughter and her future husband will choose to give—like the poor widow, wholeheartedly and sacrificially. Lord, especially if You choose to bless _____ and _____ with abundance, I pray they would remember that everything they have is Yours. And that giving is not just about money, but everything You have blessed them with. Please help them to give generously and cheerfully, not reluctantly, of their time, talent, and treasure.

Father, a godly perspective on money and prosperity is a matter of priorities and values. In fact, You encouraged us to anchor our treasures in heaven and assured us in the greatest sermon ever preached, the Sermon on the Mount, that where our treasures are, our hearts will be as well (Matthew 6:20–21). And so it is my prayer that both _____ and _____ would eagerly and joyfully store up treasures in heaven.

Protect them from the emptiness that comes from pursuing and coveting worldly gain. Lord, please help them to be mindful of the deceitfulness of riches, and the inflated ego and false sense of meaning or value that can come with wealth. Father, grant them obedient and humble hearts and a keen sense of responsibility to use whatever they are given for You and Your kingdom.

Heavenly Father, weddings can be very expensive. From the flowers and decorations to the entertainment and honeymoon—it all adds up. And just because you have money doesn't mean you should spend it frivolously. Please give my daughter and future son-in-law the grace to stand against worldly pressure. Lord, please protect _____ and _____ from thinking that they have to spend an exorbitant amount of money in order to have a beautiful wedding. Give them the wisdom to spend money where it needs to be spent and the confidence that their wedding will be amazing no matter what.

As husband and wife, it is important that _____ and _____ make unified financial decisions. Lord, please give them the wisdom and humility to do so. Teach them to love, respect, and support one another as they decide how they will spend money. Help them to be on the lookout for the enemy who would love to use money to drive a wedge between them. Please guide them as they try to navigate through any sort of financial debt. Lord, keep them from being overwhelmed and teach them to submit everything to You.

Lord, I also pray that they would not just tithe, but that they would give cheerfully, passionately, and generously—to charity foundations, ministries, and those with needs in their lives. Help them see the opportunities around them to bless others in Your name so that their actions can be an expression of Your love and generosity.

Above all, may they remember that it is more blessed to give than to receive (Acts 20:35). You have challenged us to "Give, and it will be given to you. A good measure, pressed down, shaken together and running over, will be poured into your lap. For with the measure you use, it will be measured to you" (Luke 6:38). Lord, please help them to give generously like You do.

In Jesus's name, amen.

. . . .

Remember this: Whoever sows sparingly will also reap sparingly,
and whoever sows generously will also reap generously.
Each of you should give what you have decided in your heart to give,
not reluctantly or under compulsion, for God loves a cheerful giver.
2 CORINTHIANS 9:6–7

Keep your lives free from the love of money and be content
with what you have, because God has said,
"Never will I leave you; never will I forsake you."
HEBREWS 13:5

Lord,

Thank You for the gift of laughter. Everyone loves a good laugh. At first glance, laughter doesn't come across as something especially meaningful to pray about. It is not a common topic preached from the pulpit or discussed at Bible study. And it does not seem as if it can have a significant impact on relationships or life in general. And yet, laughter matters, because You have a sense of humor and felt that it was important enough to give us the gift of laughter. Not only that, just as everyone has been given a unique set of fingerprints, no two people on the planet have the same laugh. Like the rising and setting of the sun, the ability to laugh declares Your glory in its own unique and beautiful way!

To truly enjoy having fun and laughing together, _____ and _____ need deep, abiding joy and a sincere and solid friendship. Lord, I pray that they would be best friends, sharing an intimacy and trust that only comes through You. Give them a godly friendship anchored in Your love, protection, and faithfulness. Heavenly Father, I pray that they would enjoy a covenant loyalty and friendship that mirrors their friendship with You.

Help them to seek Your heart for the meaning of friendship and joy in their marriage. That not only would they be intimate lovers, but faithful friends as well. As they walk in joy and friendship, I pray that they would have countless moments filled with laughter. Let laughter fill their home and cause them to praise and thank You.

Heavenly Father, I pray that _____ and _____ would be joyful always and laugh often. In those moments when life seems mundane and monotonous, please help them to appreciate and cherish the moments when they get to laugh out loud together. Every good and perfect gift comes from

You, Lord. Bless this beloved couple with a sense of humor that honors You. Keep them from taking life too seriously and becoming overly dramatic and analytical. As often as possible, please bless them with the gift of a deep belly laugh, the kind of laughter that sets tears rolling down their cheeks.

Lord, life is full of hardships and heartbreak. You never intended for us to live comfortable lives, but told us that we would experience trouble as we journey through life. As Your children, my daughter and her fiancé are being transformed and conformed every day into the image of Christ. While this is the highest calling, it is also the greatest challenge. More than likely, they will walk through seasons filled with one trial after another. Lord, please bless them with lighthearted, joy-filled moments to help them persevere. Remind them that although weeping may endure for a night, joy comes in the morning—joy wrapped up in the promise that someday there will be no more tears or pain! Thank You, Father.

Lord, _____ and _____ have a lot going on as they prepare for their wedding. Please turn any stress or frustration into thanksgiving and joy. Turn their joy into laughter and let it be contagious, so that everyone around them is blessed. Father, I pray that when people witness their joy, they would see Your joy. Please bless them with an amazing wedding day filled with love, joy, and a lot of laughter.

In Jesus's name, amen.

. . . .

Light shines on the righteous and joy on the upright in heart.
PSALM 97:11

Challenge #3

We're all given a finite number of twenty-four-hour days. Your challenge for today is to set aside fifteen minutes. Yes, just fifteen. Do whatever you have to do to make the time and take the time. If you're already thinking about how hard it's going to be to set aside fifteen minutes from your congested schedule, you're not alone. My life seems like I am always running on empty; I always have more to do than I have time or energy to do it. That is an especially daunting reality right now in the midst of planning Erin's wedding. As exciting as it all is, it's also time consuming and, dare I say, exhausting. But, as the saying goes, we make time for what matters most.

So, during the fifteen minutes you have set aside, I want you to simply thank God. Don't ask Him for anything, don't worry, don't complain—just spend this time being still and uncluttered so you can thank Him for who He is and all that He has done for you and your family.

Personally, it helps me to write out my prayers. If you'd like to do the same, have a pen and journal handy so you can commit everything to the page as well. It's amazing how your perspective and heart can change when you take the time to be grateful and thank God. He has blessed us beyond measure, and we don't tell Him enough how thankful we are.

$$Tip \#3$$

There is no way to get around the fact that a wedding is an enormous investment. It's an emotional investment of two people's lives, and their investment deeply impacts the lives of those who love them. A wedding demands vulnerability due to the investment of your heart, emotions, and even dreams as the journey toward tomorrow begins anew for the whole family. In addition, it is a significant investment of time, money, and energy. Lastly, it is an investment of prayer—which I believe is the most important one of all because it comes from the deepest recesses of the heart and soul.

Early in the planning process for Erin's wedding, we realized we needed to decide what our investment priorities would be. You can spend a lot of money on cool and meaningful things, but just because you *can* do something does not necessarily mean you *should* do it—or that the Lord is leading you to do it. God often strives to teach us temperance, restraint, and good stewardship, as opposed to excess.

In fact, good stewardship leads us to invest in what will last rather than what is temporary. For example, flowers are an important and beautiful part of a wedding, but they won't last very long, so our investment in them will reflect that value. On the other hand, capturing treasured moments through photographs and video will allow the wedding to endure for generations. Accordingly, it will bless our grandchildren one day, when they watch their parents' wedding ceremony and reception. What a rich, rewarding legacy to invest in.

Investing must be both reality driven and value driven; in other words, invest in your priorities. Certainly, as two young people prepare for a wedding, marriage, and new life together, an investment in prayer for them is an investment in both time and eternity. What you choose to invest in is your decision, and it will clearly reflect what you feel is most important. When deciding what wedding needs will require more investment than others, my counsel is to pray first and ask God to help you choose wisely; that way you'll end up spending wisely as well.

Father,

The topic of priorities is really about value—in other words, whatever holds the most value to us becomes what is most important in our lives. More often than not, we govern our decisions based upon our values and prioritize accordingly. What we care about and value most, we make a top priority. And usually, those top priorities get most of our time, talent, and treasure. In a world filled with temptations and distractions, it is easy for our priorities to get messed up. But, for those who know and love Jesus, finding our way back to what is most valuable is only a prayer away.

Lord, love means so much to You—so much that Your Word declares emphatically that without love, we are nothing. So, Father, more than anything, I pray that You would be _____ and _____'s first love and priority, their greatest treasure. I pray that knowing and loving You more and more each day would be their heart's deepest desire, and that their love for You would move them to great faith, obedience, and love for others.

My prayer for my daughter and her fiancé is that their priorities would follow Yours. That what has value to You would shape that which has value to them. Father, You made our highest good Your priority and sent Your Son to save us at such a great cost. I pray that my daughter and future son-in-law would do the same and place the highest good of others above their own. Above convenience, comfort, dreams, passions, and everything else.

Lord, let them carefully and continuously assess their priorities that they might diligently keep their priorities pleasing to You. The world, the flesh, and the devil constantly wear away at heavenly priorities and values. Help them to remember what is most important and be quick to repent should either of them step off the path You have chosen for them. Give them godly counsel and friends to speak into their lives should either of them compromise their priorities, and grant them eyes to see and ears to hear godly admonition.

Lord, the closer we get to this wedding, the more decisions they have to make. As _____ and _____ make these decisions, please help them focus on You, their greatest priority. Please be honored and glorified in every choice they make so that their wedding day will reflect their love for You and each other.

I pray these things in Jesus's name, amen.

· ·

[Jesus] answered, "Love the Lord your God with all your heart
and with all your soul and with all your strength
and with all your mind"; and, "Love your neighbor as yourself."

LUKE 10:27

Blessed is the one who does not walk in step with the wicked or stand
in the way that sinners take or sit in the company of mockers,
but whose delight is in the law of the LORD, and who meditates
on his law day and night. That person is like a tree planted
by streams of water, which yields its fruit in season
and whose leaf does not wither—whatever they do prospers.

PSALM 1:1-3

Heavenly Father,

If there is a word that describes Your love for us, it is *sacrificial.* You gave up everything because You love us more than we can comprehend. Through Your perfect, unconditional love, Jesus lived a life of complete surrender, sacrificing His life so that we might live. Amazingly, You have called us to walk in that same love and reach out to that same world, so they might not perish but have eternal life. And even more amazing, You've empowered and filled us with the same Spirit, so that we can love sacrificially like You do.

Father, this kind of love cannot reach to the world without sacrifice. You were unwavering in Mark 10:45, when You told us that the Son of Man did not come to be served, but to serve. And You are still in this world to serve others sacrificially through those who believe. We are here to serve, not be served. We are Your hands, Your feet, Your voice.

Father, it is my prayer that _____ and _____ would have the passion and vision to love and serve You and others sacrificially and selflessly. I want them to know the unspeakable joy of putting You first, others second, and themselves last. Lord, a servant's heart must begin in their home—so I ask that they would serve one another sacrificially and selflessly, with joy, purpose, and humility. Father, I pray that they would each put the other ahead of themselves—ahead of their own wants, dreams, and desires. That their love for one another would be selfless and generous, and that all the godly attributes described in 1 Corinthians chapter 13 would find their fulfillment in her love toward him, and his love toward her, and in the way each of them loves You.

Lord, as they go out into the world, I pray that _____ and _____ would walk in Your sacrificial, no-strings-attached, unconditional love as they relate to the people in their lives. Please bless them with a sense of purpose to give as You gave, to live unto Christ, and die to themselves. Father, I pray that You would show them the way to lose their lives for the sake of serving Your kingdom. Teach them how to give from the heart and truly expect nothing in return. I pray that their reward would be in pleasing You and walking in joy-filled obedience, becoming more like Jesus every single day.

God, please help my daughter and future son-in-law to hold on loosely to the treasures and distractions of this world and cling to You instead. Father, there is no substitute for Your priceless love; it is the only thing that can fill an empty soul. The world is filled with imitations and counterfeits. I pray _____ and _____ would do whatever You call them to do to bring You glory, and sacrificially and selflessly show others that Your love is real.

In Jesus's name, amen.

. . . .

Give, and it will be given to you.
A good measure, pressed down, shaken together
and running over, will be poured into your lap.
For with the measure you use, it will be measured to you.

LUKE 6:38

Dear Father,

You know better than anyone else that freedom is not free because You paid its price—a price we could never pay. The freedom that we enjoy as Your children cost You everything. It cost You Your one and only Son—Jesus. No man can earn his own freedom, it is a gift! And as such, it can only be received and unwrapped as we are set free. Your Word declares that "if the Son sets you free, you will be free indeed" (John 8:36). No one can experience authentic, lasting liberty without Jesus. He is the truth, and the truth sets us free when we continue in His Word (John 8:31–32).

As the mother of the bride, Lord, I long for You to show my daughter and her fiancé what it means to be truly free through the freedom Christ purchased for those who love Him. Please give them wisdom, discernment, and insight so they can differentiate between what the world calls freedom and the true and lasting freedom that You have given them through Your Spirit. They are already free! They have been set free from sin, and nothing and no one can hold them captive or keep them from You and Your perfect love. The enemy is relentless, but he is no match for the Lord of lords. Remind _____ and _____ of their position and what they possess as children of Your covenant, so they can walk in complete freedom.

Lord, the gift of freedom can open doors to bring You glory and share the hope we have in Christ. I pray that You would allow _____ and _____ to pray bold prayers, so that they can be used by You to freely share the gospel and their love for Jesus wherever they go. As they continue their journey through life, keep them from the temptation to misuse or even abuse the freedom they have in Christ. Keep them from being tempted to use it to their own advantage. Instead, bless them with the grace to be ever diligent in protecting the gift of freedom so that they might live to please and honor You above all else.

Father, grant them the insight and conviction to differentiate between their *rights* and their *responsibilities* with respect to freedom. Help them to see that even though they have the right to exercise their freedom in any number of ways, they also have the responsibility to use it to accomplish Your will. Help them to embrace the highest levels of accountability, to pursue integrity in their freedom, and to never allow it to stand above the One who sets them free.

Lord, I pray that _____ and _____ would grow and mindfully heed the life lessons You bring into their lives. Help them learn everything You desire to teach them, so they can live abundantly and flourish in the freedom You have so graciously provided.

In Jesus's name, amen.

· ·

You, my brothers and sisters, were called to be free.
But do not use your freedom to indulge the flesh;
rather, serve one another humbly in love.
For the entire law is fulfilled in keeping this one command:
"Love your neighbor as yourself."

GALATIANS 5:13–14

Dear God,

When things are going the way we want them to, *courage* is just a word used to describe superheroes. It is not needed or talked about when life is smooth and easy. But when we face pain, chaos, the unexpected, or heartbreaking circumstances, the reality of our need for courage becomes crystal clear. And our need for courage always leads us to our greater need—more of You.

As we pray and plan for _____ and _____'s wedding and their life together, the last thing I want to think about is something going wrong. But the reality is, it's quite likely that something will not go as we've planned. We live in an imperfect, fallen world filled with imperfect, fallen people. Although we hope and pray for the best, hardship and pain are usually right around the corner.

Father, Your Word even tells us that we will experience trouble in this life. But the good news is that You are God . . . and You are good. You have conquered the enemy and overcome this world and, because of what You have done, we have everything we need to live courageously by faith. Thank You, Lord!

Father, as my daughter and her fiancé pray, plan, and prepare, would You please grant them the courage to live for You regardless of their circumstances? Help them to deny themselves, take up their cross, and follow You. Give them courage to take the high road and turn from the easy path, regardless of the cost. I pray that they would walk courageously and turn away from all worldly temptation and fear. God, remind them of Your constant presence. They are never alone. You go before them, and You will neither leave them nor forsake them.

Lord, in the face of fearful circumstances, it takes courage to pray and wait. We wait for You to do what only You can do. When my daughter and her husband-to-be are tempted to take matters into their own hands, please remind them to seek You and wait for wisdom, guidance, and direction. You see the big picture and how all the pieces of our lives fall into place. Help them to be patient and trust that in Your perfect timing, You will move on their behalf and work all things together for good.

Heavenly Father, please give _____ and _____ the courage to love You more than the praise of people, to kneel before You in humility so they can stand strong in every circumstance, and to surrender their dreams to live for Yours. Bless them with the spiritual resolve to allow their hearts to be broken by the things that break Your heart, so that their lives would be a courageous witness and example of Your power, goodness, and love.

In Jesus's name, amen.

. . . .

Have I not commanded you? Be strong and courageous.
Do not be afraid; do not be discouraged,
for the LORD your God will be with you wherever you go.
JOSHUA 1:9

What, then, shall we say in response to these things?
If God is for us, who can be against us?
ROMANS 8:31

O Lord,

You are the source of all compassion and the God of all comfort. You are kind, gracious, patient, and merciful. You promise to never leave us nor forsake us. You comfort us during life's trials and heartbreaks. You are trustworthy and dependable. You always keep Your promises; You do what You say You're going to do. Thank You for providing everything we need to survive and thrive as we live one day at a time upon the earth.

Heavenly Father, sin has caused humankind to pervert the beauty and goodness of everything You have created. As a result of the fall of man, the world can be harsh and unforgiving. The Bible tells us that we will all experience trouble as we journey through life. No one is exempt (John 16:33). People are hurting, and life is hard. But circumstances can be overwhelming even when life is easy. The best of intentions can sometimes result in discouraging outcomes, too. We need You, Lord. Every hour of every day, we need You.

There will likely be difficult days ahead as _____ and _____ prepare to get married and strive to do Your will in their lives. There will be days when they feel like all hope, life, and joy have been sucked out of them. Moments when battling the world, the flesh, and the devil take a severe toll. Lord, only You know for certain, but they might even have to endure seasons of unexpected heartbreak and pain. I pray they will not have to experience any of this, but if they do, please help them to seek You immediately for comfort and compassion. Father, keep them from defaulting to their own solutions, their own strength, and their own big ideas. Help them to remember that all the good and godly works in the world are no substitute for the perfect will of God.

Heavenly Father, You are our strong shelter from the raging storms of life, our constant refuge in times of trouble. Reveal Your power and presence when _____ and _____ feel as though they're being pulled under by waves of adversity. Give them patience, understanding, and empathy. Show them how to comfort one another, especially when it is hardest to do so.

Father, with the comfort You graciously extend to them, I pray that they would comfort others. There will be people in their lives who need a listening ear and a shoulder to cry on. Please fill _____ and _____ with Your endless supply of compassion so that they willingly and sacrificially comfort those in need.

In Jesus's name, amen.

. . . .

Praise be to the God and Father of our Lord Jesus Christ,
the Father of compassion and the God of all comfort,
who comforts us in all our troubles, so that we can comfort
those in any trouble with the comfort we ourselves receive from God.
For just as we share abundantly in the sufferings of Christ,
so also our comfort abounds through Christ.

2 CORINTHIANS 1:3-5

Challenge #4

Today's challenge is personal. Whether we like it or not, our daughters have been watching us for as long as they have been alive. You and I have been living examples to our girls.

Your daughter, the bride-to-be, has watched the way you have lived your life much more closely than she has listened to anything you have said. Yes, the good, the bad, and the ugly. No worries, that's not what this is about. Besides, the grace and forgiveness of God covers all that.

One of the ways your example impacts your daughter's life is through the way you treat your husband, her father. This book is about preparing your daughter to be a bride and wife through prayer, so today is the day you love your daughter by praying specifically for her father. Maybe you pray for him all the time or maybe you don't. Maybe you have a thriving, healthy marriage, or maybe you're divorced and, honestly, the thought of praying for your daughter's father turns your stomach. Maybe your daughter is adopted. Regardless of the circumstances, today is the day to bless your daughter by praying for her dad or the most significant male or father figure in her life. The harder it is for you to do this, the greater the blessing will be for all of you.

If your daughter's father is no longer alive, allow me to suggest that you spend this time praying for your future son-in-law—that God would prepare him even now to be a godly father and example to your future grandchildren. Did I just say *grandchildren*? Yes, please!

Tip #4

Whether we like it or not, we live in a technology-driven, Internet and social media–saturated cyber culture. If you need information regarding just about anything, all you have to do is Google it or find a search app.

Easy access to a plethora of information can be a huge blessing; it can make life considerably easier when planning a wedding. However, for the mother of the bride, it can also be overwhelming and intimidating. Fear not, my friend; I'm here for you. I've got this covered.

From venue options and videographers to reception etiquette and wedding dresses, I have been there and done that. Since we've started this journey, I have had no shortage of nights when I've fallen asleep with a wedding planning book, laptop, or cell phone in hand. I did the research so that you don't have to. Well, sort of . . .

No two weddings are alike. Just like your daughter is unique, so will her wedding be a one-of-a-kind celebration, so these are only recommendations. You might find other blogs, websites, and apps that are more useful for you and your daughter. But here are some to get you started:

- *Pinterest.* Erin loves Pinterest (www.pinterest.com). In fact, she has "pinned" just about everything—from wedding ideas to her future home and all things baby. I try not to spend much time there because I get sucked in, if you know what I mean. It happens to the best of us, doesn't it?

- *Blogs/Websites.* Here are the wedding sites I chose to follow and where I found a ton of helpful and creative ideas and information. Just Google them for their links:
  - The Knot
  - Wedding Wire
  - Wedding Chicks
  - Bridal Musings
  - Style Me Pretty
  - Wedding Photo Inspiration
  - Magnolia Rouge
  - Trendy Bride Magazine
  - Best Wedding Shots
  - 100LayerCake
  - June Bug Weddings
  - The Bride Collection

- *Phone Apps.* There are a lot of helpful phone applications. Here are the ones that I used:
  - Red Stamp Cards
  - Wedding Planner by The Knot
  - Paperless Post
  - Countdown

- *Inspirational Instagram and Twitter sites.* We all need to be inspired and encouraged daily, but especially while planning for a wedding. Here are some of the sites that I follow. I hope they bless you like they have me.

  Instagram:
  - Jesus Calling
  - GodlyladyTalk
  - Undisputed Faith
  - Christian Soulmates
  - Trust God Bro
  - Jesus Centric
  - Christian Worship
  - InstaGod Ministries
  - Desiring God

  Twitter:
  - @JesusGraces
  - @PrayinFaith
  - @BookOProverbs
  - @Jesus_Calling
  - @GodPosts
  - @Godly_Life
  - @ArmorOGod
  - @LovLikeJesus

Lord,

We were created to honor and glorify You. One beautiful way we can do this is through abiding in You so that we bear the fruit of the Spirit—love, joy, peace, patience, kindness, goodness, faithfulness, gentleness, and self-control. As _____ and _____ prepare their hearts for the covenant of marriage and as their relationship with You continues to grow, I pray that what You have planted in them will mature and bear good fruit. Not just fruit that will be evident today, but fruit that will endure the storms of life and last forever.

As John 13:35 explains, people will know that we are Yours by our love. Heavenly Father, because of Your love, we can know and experience true love. Because of Your love, we have the great privilege to love You and others. As _____ and _____ prepare to get married, fill them afresh with Your all-consuming love and cause them to love each other in a more profound, sacrificial, and meaningful way. Father, help them grasp how vast and far-reaching the love of Christ is, and help them truly understand that there is nothing greater than to know this love—Your love, which surpasses knowledge.

Real joy and peace have nothing to do with circumstances. Lord, I pray that Your abiding joy and peace will be evident in _____ and _____'s lives, regardless of what they walk through in the days leading up to their wedding and for the many years following. Your Word says to "let the peace of Christ rule in your hearts" (Colossians 3:15). We live in a world full of confusion, hatred, unrest, and turmoil. Regardless of what happens around them, let Your perfect peace rule in their hearts and help them to be joyful and filled with gratitude.

Lord, You alone are good. During this time of preparation, please flood _____ and _____ with Your goodness so that all that is good, pure, and holy flows from their lives into the world around them. I pray that their good deeds would be a response to and reflection of their love for You and the goodness You have planted in their hearts.

When I think about patience, kindness, faithfulness, and gentleness, I think of You, Jesus, and Your willingness to humble Yourself in every way. By Your presence and power in their lives, both my daughter and her soon-to-be husband can choose to do the same—to humble themselves, be faithful, gracious, gentle, and kind to each other and others. This practice is not always easy, and it's often costly. We all have bad days; we might be caught off guard by the unexpected, and sometimes we face intense, heartbreaking trials. Lord, I pray that kindness, patience, and gentleness would mark the way for them to live a loving, God-fearing lifestyle.

We all tend to be selfish at times. We want our own way, and we choose the shortcuts in life rather than walking the extra mile. Father, when _____ and _____ are tempted to walk in the flesh rather than the power of the Holy Spirit, when they are enticed to sidestep Your perfect will, please remind them to be self-controlled and wise. Help them to seek You and trust that You will enable them to be obedient and self-disciplined. Work in their hearts so they submit to You in their motives, thoughts, words, and deeds.

Father, thank You that _____ and _____ don't have to earn or produce the fruit of the Spirit by their own strength or effort. Through their relationship with You and as they abide in Christ, they have been given everything they need for life and godliness. As Your chosen people, You have clothed my daughter and her fiancé with compassion, kindness, humility, gentleness, and patience. Thank You, Lord!

In Jesus's name, amen.

* *

Live a life worthy of the Lord and please him in every way.
COLOSSIANS 1:10

TIME

Father,

Just as you know the number of hairs on our heads, You've already determined the sum total of our heartbeats and breaths upon this earth. Eternity endures forever, but a lifetime is limited to years, hours, and minutes. The number of days we are given may be brief or encompass many years, but no matter how long we live, life is short compared to eternity.

More than anything, Lord, I pray that _____ and _____ will live with the knowledge that tomorrow is not promised to anyone and that every heartbeat is a gift for the glory of God. Help them to be ever mindful that You created time, and You care about how they spend it. We can get so caught up in our own lives and the cares of this world that we think twenty-four hours is not enough. Please remind _____ and _____ that You determined the exact number of hours per day and minutes per hour because You're God, and You know exactly what we need.

What we do as we pass through time shapes the eternal legacy we leave behind. Please give my daughter and her fiancé vision, motivation, and compassion to care about the things You care about. Motivate and inspire them to put people, spreading the gospel, and kingdom work above their own comfort, pleasure, and prosperity. Help them to use their time wisely as they choose Your will above their own. And, Father, please keep them from being so busy that they forget to spend time with You and each other.

Lord, please bless _____ and _____ with discernment and wisdom so they can recognize when this world tries to give them a false sense of security. Remind them of what Your Word says in 1 John 2:17, "The world and its desires pass away, but whoever does the will of God lives forever." Help them anchor their souls to this reality even though time appears as though it will march on forever. Teach them to appreciate the breadth of life no matter how well everything seems to be going or how strong and healthy they may be.

Father, You determined before _____ and _____ were born that this would be an exciting time for them. This season of preparation will go by much faster than they think it will. Amid all the excitement and decision making, it's easy to get distracted and bogged down by all the details. Lord, please help them make the most of the time You have given them during this season. Getting married happens once in a lifetime, so please help them to take it all in and enjoy everything, one moment and day at a time.

Heavenly Father, I pray that as they pass through this life, _____ and _____ would be good stewards of the time You have graciously granted them by using every moment to honor You and impact eternity.

In Jesus's name, amen.

. . . .

You see, at just the right time, when we were still powerless,
Christ died for the ungodly.
ROMANS 5:6

He has made everything beautiful in its time.
He has also set eternity in the human heart; yet no one
can fathom what God has done from beginning to end.
ECCLESIASTES 3:11

SEX AND AFFECTION

Heavenly Father,

What beautiful and mysterious gifts sex and affection are! Lord, You have given us these gifts in the covenant of marriage, in order that we might know one another and express love in a deeper, more intimate way.

It's sad that in today's world the gift of sex has become more about selfishness and abuse than the holy gift You created.

Lord, my prayer for _____ and _____ is that Your original intent for sex and affection would be fully and passionately understood and embraced. Father, protect them from the temptations and perversions of this fallen world. Let them always experience and appreciate the beauty and depth of true intimacy. Please allow them to enjoy the mystery of becoming one physically, emotionally, and spiritually. Lord, protect their intimacy through the gift of unconditional love and trust.

God, nothing else reaches so deeply into our inmost beings and touches us the way loving and meaningful sex does. Neither can anything else cut or hurt as deeply as loveless and meaningless sex can. The potential for damage is far reaching. Father, please guard _____ and _____ from meaningless, inappropriate sex. Keep the temptation to desire sex or affection outside of their marriage far from them. Help them to be tender, affectionate, and sexually attracted to each other throughout their entire lives. Lord, I pray that their love for each other would never grow cold.

Father, I pray that _____ and _____ would be confident in their sexuality and body perception. Help them to be open, honest, and vulnerable, so that nothing hidden would harm their love for each other. Encourage them to explore a depth of intimacy with each other that only You can provide. Help them to treat sex as the priceless treasure You intended it to be and never abuse or misuse it for selfish purposes. Give them the courage and determination to resist every form of temptation that would distort or come against true intimacy. Lord, keep their physical relationship alive and active and keep them from getting bored or complacent.

Heavenly Father, by Your grace, I pray that _____ and _____ will experience sex, affection, and a depth of intimacy with each other that only You can give them. May they grow in their relationship with You—knowing You more and more—so that they can experience a greater knowledge of each other and intimacy as a married couple. Thank You, Lord.

In Jesus's name, amen.

. . . .

That is why a man leaves his father and mother
and is united to his wife, and they become one flesh.
GENESIS 2:24

A wife of noble character who can find?
She is worth far more than rubies.
Her husband has full confidence in her
and lacks nothing of value.
PROVERBS 31:10-11

Heavenly Father,

Before we were born, You saw our unformed bodies and tenderly knit us together in our mothers' wombs. You determined and orchestrated every single detail, including the color of our eyes, our unique DNA and fingerprints, even the exact number of hairs on our heads. The human body is amazing! The complexities and intricate details of how our bodies function point to Your creativity and majesty.

Lord, You are a God of order. You created the human body so that all of our body parts work together in a synchronized, orderly fashion. If just one part of the body is injured, diseased, disabled, or out of sync, the rest of the body knows and often works to heal and compensate for that particular body part. The body displays Your glory, power, and purpose in such a profound way.

Father, _____ and _____ are fearfully and wonderfully made. You created and know every inch of their bodies. From the top of their heads to the bottom of their feet and every awesome detail in between, You see it all. Thank You for giving _____ and _____ life and breath. Thank You for blessing them with hearts that beat and brains that function according to Your divine design.

Lord, because of the plethora of ever-changing information and products and services available, it is easy to get confused and fearful regarding what is healthy and good for you and what isn't. Please bless _____ and _____ with wisdom, understanding, clarity, and conviction when it comes to what to eat and how to take care of their bodies. Keep them from becoming too consumed or obsessed with health care, wellness, and fitness. Help them to remember that while all these things are good, they should not distract or keep them from their first love, You.

You have given my daughter and her fiancé everything they need for life and godliness. Father, You know what is best for them. Help them to seek You first for all their health care needs. If at any point there is a concern that must be dealt with, please send them to the doctors or specialists that You want them to see. Guide them in the direction You want them to go so they can receive the answers they need and the best care available.

God, as You know, there are countless sicknesses and diseases in this fallen world. If my daughter or son-in-law must walk through a season of poor health, bless them with Your peace that surpasses understanding. If they must suffer and endure great hardship due to sickness, in Jesus's name, please strengthen and protect them. If something serious is wrong, help them to not be anxious or fearful, but to cry out to You for comfort and healing. Help them to trust You completely. Remind them that, no matter what kind of news or diagnosis a doctor or report gives them, You are God. You heal and You perform miracles. Because of who You are, they always have hope.

Lord, I pray that _____ and _____ will never have to walk through any life-threatening diseases. Please bless them with good health so that they can love and serve You until they're old and gray.

In Jesus's name, amen.

. . . .

Then they cried to the LORD in their trouble, and he saved them
from their distress. He sent out his word and healed them;
he rescued them from the grave.

PSALM 107:19–20

Heavenly Father,

It is hard to even think about suffering and trials when we are so focused on the joys of wedding planning and the blessing of marriage. And yet, Lord, the truth is, _____ and _____ will experience suffering, trials, heartbreak, and grief on this side of eternity. In this sin-drenched, fallen world, we all suffer. But You have promised that even though we will have trouble and great tribulation in this world, we can have peace and confidence because You have overcome the world (John 16:33). Thank You, Jesus!

Though difficult to understand, Your approach to suffering and the profound way You use trials to accomplish Your will is awesome. Not one of my daughter and her fiancé's troubles or tears have been or will be wasted. You work all things together for their good and Your glory. Thank You, Father!

Lord, You led a life of suffering. You were "despised and rejected by mankind, a man of suffering, and familiar with pain" (Isaiah 53:3). It is amazing and humbling to me that You never took any shortcuts or the easy way out. And although You were fully God, You were completely human. You understand and can relate to our struggles and heartbreak, because "we do not have a high priest who is unable to empathize with our weaknesses, but we have one who has been tempted in every way, just as we are—yet he did not sin" (Hebrews 4:15). This is so comforting.

Every human being has burdens to bear. Thank You for caring about each one of us as if we were Your only child. Thank You! Father, I pray for this couple because trials and suffering will find them. Please strengthen and protect them from the pressures that come with trials, pressures that would try to confuse, divide, or drive a wedge between them. Lord, help them to surrender and come to You, so that amid whatever storm they are in, they will find refuge and safety. Use their burdens to bring them closer together and closer to You.

Please God, help them to be patient, to trust You in the fires of adversity. As they suffer through heartbreak, help them not just endure but triumph over everything they go through. Heavenly Father, give _____ and _____ the patience and power to persevere, to seek Your glory no matter what. Through the trials, hardships, and pain, please comfort and remind them that suffering will not last forever; it's a season that will eventually come to an end.

Your Word is clear that there is a relationship between suffering and glory. As hard as this is to comprehend, please help them humbly submit to this reality. Grant them grace to grow and persevere in their trials, just as Romans 5:3 encourages us to "glory in our sufferings, because we know that suffering produces perseverance." First Peter 4:13 further instructs us to "rejoice inasmuch as [we] participate in the sufferings of Christ, so that [we] may be overjoyed when his glory is revealed." Father, it is hard to rejoice in the valley of suffering. This is not something that my daughter and her future husband can do in their own strength, so I'm asking You to help them focus, not on their trials and suffering, but on You so they can choose to rejoice in You no matter what.

Lord, remind them to use the sword of the Spirit and to walk in the Word. Please teach them to be aware and vigilant, to watch for the enemy, just as 1 Peter 5:8 warns: "Be alert and of sober mind. Your enemy the devil prowls around like a roaring lion looking for someone to devour." Help them to remember that the way of the cross is not a life of comfort and ease and that this world is a battleground, not a playground. Father, please help _____ and _____ to not be surprised when trials come into their lives but to remember that every trial has a purpose. You see and know every detail, and You promise that victory is coming. Victory will come because the battle has always been and will always be Yours! Thank You, Father.

In Jesus's name, amen.

. . . .

[Paul and Barnabas] strengthened the believers
and encouraged them to remain true to the faith.
"We must pass through many troubles to enter
the Kingdom of God," they taught.

ACTS 14:21–22 GNT

Our present sufferings are not worth comparing
with the glory that will be revealed in us.

ROMANS 8:18

It's challenge time again. Here's what I would like for you to consider doing: Prayerfully search out seven passages of Scripture that have a unique application to your daughter, her growth as a godly young woman, and her impending wedding. Jot each of them down separately, then explain why you feel they are relevant to her at this time in her life. Put them in separate envelopes. When they are ready, give them to your daughter—you can do this either one at a time or all together. You decide how and when to give her the Scripture messages but make sure you deliver them before the wedding.

Choosing these verses and expressing them so personally will bless your daughter as she moves ever closer to the most significant decision she has ever made. You may find they become meaningful talking points as she ponders each verse and your brief commentary on its application to her life. If you're not sure where to start, check out Proverbs 31.

*E*arly in the wedding planning process, my daughter and her fiancé had an important discussion about social media. Prior to this, Erin and I had had numerous discussions regarding the value of being deliberate and strategic when it came to sharing our lives with the world. The bottom line is this: everything you share on social media represents who you are. Before you press Send, ask yourself, *Is this who I am?* and *Does this honor God?*

When deciding on whether to post something on social media, it's also important to remember that what you do or say reflects and affects not only you but the people you love as well—your family. Once you put it out there in cyberspace, you can't take it back. Of course, you can delete a Facebook or Instagram post or tweet, but you never know who might have read what you shared before you decided to take it down. Do you really want to have to worry about all that? Instead, think (and pray) before you post.

For my daughter's wedding, we decided that certain aspects of the celebration should be kept private. Because of the number of people invited, we had to be gracious and purposeful in how we approached our guests about their social media wedding postings. After much thought and consideration, we decided that the wedding ceremony would be kept private.

What *private* means to our family might be different from what it means to you and your family.

How to navigate social media is the bride and groom's decision, but no matter what they choose to do, what works for them needs to be respected and honored by everyone involved.

Father,

I am amazed by the depth and breadth of Your love and tender care for us. You made a covenant of love that You continue to protect and keep. Thank You for remaining faithful even when we are not, and for teaching us by Your perfect example what faithfulness is all about. From Your love and commitment to our highest good comes Your protection and provision. From our daily bread to the eternal salvation of our souls, we have everything we need. Thank You, Lord!

God, I pray that my daughter and her fiancé would understand that there is no safer place on the planet than under the shelter of Your wings. You assure them of Your protection and provision as they live their lives for You, one breath at a time, one prayer at a time.

I pray that _____ and _____ would realize that their need to be protected and provided for will find its fulfillment in You and Your will. You are the Bread of Life, and when they pray for You to give them their daily bread (Luke 11:3), it is You they need more than anything else in this world. You sustain their lives and nourish their souls. You *are* life, just as Colossians 3:4 declares, "When Christ, who is your life, appears, then you also will appear with him in glory."

Lord, our needs are often subjective, defined by selfish and worldly perspectives. Please help _____ and _____ seek You first and grasp the reality that You know what they need—not only before they ask, but in what constitutes a true need. Heavenly Father, when they feel as though their needs have not been met, please help them trust Your judgment and remember what James said: "Every good and perfect gift is from above, coming down from the Father of the heavenly lights, who does not change like shifting shadows" (James 1:17). You never change. You are the same yesterday, today, and forever. You will never withhold something from them unless their need for what You want to give them is greater.

Remind them, especially during times of crisis, that what they perceive as a need may not be what they need at all. They may need the grace to accept an intense trial even though they believe they should be delivered from that trial. You know what will bring them closer to You and help form Christ in their hearts. Lord, please help _____ and _____ trust in Your care. Let the words of the apostle Paul in Philippians 4:19 encourage them and give them confidence: "My God will meet all your needs according to the riches of his glory in Christ Jesus."

Heavenly Father, where You guide, You provide. Thank You, Lord! Please help my daughter and my future son-in-law take Your deeply comforting words in Luke 11:11–13 to heart: "Which of you fathers, if your son asks for a fish, will give him a snake instead? Or if he asks for an egg, will give him a scorpion? If you then, though you are evil, know how to give good gifts to your children, how much more will your Father in heaven give the Holy Spirit to those who ask him!"

Yes, Lord, remind them that You are the God of abundance and so much more.

In Jesus's beautiful name, amen.

. . . .

Do not fear, for I am with you; do not be dismayed, for I am your God.
I will strengthen you and help you;
I will uphold you with my righteous right hand.

ISAIAH 41:10

Lord,

Victory might not always look the way _____ and _____ imagine or expect. It's not about crossing the finish line first; it's about what happens in their lives and hearts as they run the race You marked out for them. Jesus, Your death on the cross appeared to be the ultimate defeat. Yet, in dying and rising again, You were victorious. And because of Your victory, _____ and _____ get the awesome privilege of choosing to live victoriously through a relationship with You. Thank You, Father!

Dear God, please enable _____ and _____ to experience the abundant joy and peace that comes with knowing that the battle is not theirs but Yours—and that You've already won! In Christ, they already have the victory. You defeated death, the grave, and the enemy. You accomplished everything that needed to be done to provide everything they would ever need in this life and for eternity.

Lord, please help them to be still and know that You are God (Psalm 46:10). Remind them that You are providing them with opportunities to know victory through living by faith and obedience. Furthermore, grant them peace that surpasses all understanding as they trust, believe, and allow You to battle for them. They need only be still, because You fight for them (Exodus 14:14).

Father, as my daughter and future son-in-law choose to follow You one day at a time, please increase their understanding and knowledge of what it means to be Yours. When life throws problems their way or when anger or stress tries to interfere and stand between them, I pray that they would turn to You for guidance and victory. Surely there will be times when the enemy will try to cause misunderstandings, hurt, and confusion, "but you give us victory over our enemies, you put our adversaries to shame" (Psalm 44:7).

When _____ and _____ choose to share their faith, they can expect resistance from the powers of darkness. But, God, You are in control. You are greater than any and every power that would try to come against them. Help them to remember 1 John 4:4: "You, dear children, are from God and have overcome them, because the one who is in you is greater than the one who is in the world." Father, help them stand in victory against the enemy by the power of Christ. Despite every form of opposition, by faith and in Your strength, let them courageously move forward in Your perfect will for their lives.

Heavenly Father, You gave us Your Word and the gift of prayer. When used together, prayer becomes a mighty weapon of righteousness. Please hide Your Word in their hearts so that their relationship with You is in sync with Your perfect plan for their lives. As time goes by, they will learn to leave their problems as well as their triumphs in Your hands. Their worries and stresses will diminish because You have prepared and trained them for life's many twists and turns. I pray that victory will prevail as _____ and _____ live their lives, leaving a legacy of love and victory for future generations to emulate.

In Jesus's name, amen.

. . . .

Everyone born of God overcomes the world.
This is the victory that has overcome the world, even our faith.
1 JOHN 5:4

Dear Lord,

Children are a gift and a beautiful heritage! As a mother, the blessings I have received through my children are endless. Thank You for entrusting me with children, Lord; children You have given me to love and lead, children who have taught me the Father-heart of God. Lord Jesus, the one word You used to describe God over and over, more than any other, was *Father*—and not just the formal word but *Abba*, or *Daddy*, a term of endearment. I realize that my children are Yours, but I want to thank You for sharing them with me and placing them in my care for however many days I have on this earth.

Please Father, as You have blessed me with children, I hope and pray that You will do the same for _____ and _____. Yes, Lord, let the joy of a child's laughter ring through their house and echo nonstop—and not merely one child, but if it is Your will, allow them to have a home filled with little ones. Please bless my daughter's womb. Keep her body free from any health issues that would make it difficult for her to get pregnant and have children. Grant this couple the opportunity to raise little ones to know and love You, Jesus. Children who will know the truth and boldly proclaim it wherever You lead them.

You already know the plans You have for _____ and _____. Plans to prosper them and not to harm them. Plans to give them great hope and a future (Jeremiah 29:11). Father, I pray that the future and good works that You have already prepared in advance for them would include children. Also, regarding children, please help _____ and _____ to surrender their hopes and dreams to Your perfect will. Heavenly Father, if Your plan includes adoption rather than biological children, or both, please allow _____ and

_____ to have open hearts and minds, and a willingness to go wherever Your Spirit leads them. Lord, as they begin to pray about having a family, prepare their hearts, one prayer at a time.

Thank You for Your Word, the best guide to parenting ever written. Please encourage my daughter and her future husband to seek You daily through reading and meditating on Scripture so they can teach and guide their children according to the truth. Father, thank You for providing everything they need to raise their children to know and love Jesus. Through the lives of their kids, help them learn how to pray boldly as they learn life lessons they cannot gain any other way.

Heavenly Father, children have so much to give and so much to teach us. Their honesty, innocence, and vulnerability—it all speaks to the character and heart of who You are, Lord. You delighted in little ones while You walked the earth; You even rejoiced when Your Father kept heavenly mysteries from the wise and revealed them to children (Matthew 11:25).

Lord, You made Your love for children evident in Matthew 19:14: "Let the little children come to me, and do not hinder them, for the kingdom of heaven belongs to such as these." I pray that my daughter and future son-in-law would have eyes to see what You saw and still see in these little ones. Truly, children are like arrows in the hands of a warrior, so please bless them with a full quiver (Psalm 127:4–5).

God, please bless _____ and _____ with the humility and ability to learn from their children and to bring them up according to their individual personalities and giftings. Lord, fill them with wisdom and show them when and how to discipline according to Your Word. Keep them from exasperating their children. Let their motives always be pure and redemptive. Father, help them to be faithful like You are and to follow through on promises and commitments they have made. Remind my daughter and future son-in-law that they themselves are imperfect. They need a Savior just as much as their children do. Please help them to be humble and to own up to their mistakes. Help them to be open and honest with their children and to seek forgiveness from them as often as they need to.

You are the ultimate example of a loving, good Father; therefore, please teach my daughter and her future husband to be loving leaders and faithful servants to their children, protecting, serving, loving, and guiding them for the brief time they remain in their care. That time will go by so quickly, but the foundation of love and faith they provide and the way they live their lives will impact their children for the rest of their lives.

In Jesus's precious and powerful name I pray, amen.

. . . .

Start children off on the way they should go,
and even when they are old they will not turn from it.
PROVERBS 22:6

The righteous lead blameless lives;
blessed are their children after them.
PROVERBS 20:7

Dear Lord,

How overwhelming it is to know that we leave a legacy every day with every decision we make. It's a legacy that will either bring You glory and honor or disappoint You; one that identifies with You or the world, backs up our talk with our walk or makes a hypocrite out of us. When it comes to a legacy, there is no middle ground, no gray area, no hiding. Our footprints follow us and show to others exactly who we are and how we have lived.

Through Adam's choice to dishonor and disobey You, sin and condemnation came into the world, deeply impacting all mankind and creation. Through Jesus's actions came salvation, freedom, hope, and eternal life for all who believe. Both left powerful legacies we can learn from.

Father, I pray that _____ and _____ would fully understand that every single day, with every choice they make, they are creating a legacy that will last far beyond their lifetimes. Help them grasp the reality that every decision matters, no matter how small or insignificant it seems. Teach them that their actions are impactful and their words have the power of life and death. Help them to rely wholly on Your grace and guidance, so they can walk in obedience.

Lord, I pray they both follow 2 Corinthians 3:2–3 and understand what Paul meant when he said, "You yourselves are our letter, written on our hearts, known and read by everyone. You show that you are a letter from Christ, the result of our ministry, written not with ink but with the Spirit of the living God, not on tablets of stone but on tablets of human hearts." I pray _____ and _____ would understand that they are living letters, written on the hearts of those whose lives they touch. Help them to be mindful that they are known and read by everyone as a letter from Christ.

_____ and _____'s wedding is part of their legacy. Whether they realize it or not, the choices they make now and how they choose to honor You as they pray, prepare, and plan will impact their lives and their legacy. It all matters. Father, please help my daughter and future son-in-law to humble themselves so they can recognize their constant need for You. No matter what decisions they have to make, please remind them to seek You first for guidance and wisdom. Keep them ever mindful that every choice they make regarding the wedding has the potential for eternal impact. Rather than be fearful or anxious, please help _____ and _____ to be passionate and excited about making choices that will shape their legacy and impact Your kingdom.

Lord, please allow _____ and _____ to live fruitful lives filled with joy and purpose. Help them love You more and love others the way You do. Father, on that great day when their lives, motives, and decisions are laid bare before You, I pray that You will be pleased—pleased with how _____ and _____ lived their lives for Your Son, Jesus, and pleased with how they chose You and Your will over the world and their own desires. I am so thankful for Your grace and mercy, Lord, for without it, _____ and _____ would not be who they are called to be, could not do what You have created them to do, and and would not leave a godly, eternal legacy of love as a result.

In Jesus's name, amen.

. . . .

We will not hide these truths from our children;
we will tell the next generation about the glorious deeds of the LORD,
about his power and his mighty wonders.

PSALM 78:4 NLT

Father,

As You know, the world is desperate for true and lasting peace. Peace that is more than just the absence of conflict. Peace that is higher and deeper, surpassing all understanding. The world longs for the kind of peace that is a manifestation of Your loving character and the fruit of Your Spirit. Peace that guards our hearts and minds.

Lord, I pray that _____ and _____ would understand that they cannot have peace in their hearts, lives, or relationships without first being connected to its source. You are the Prince of Peace. In John 15:4–5 You said, "Remain in me, as I also remain in you. No branch can bear fruit by itself; it must remain in the vine. Neither can you bear fruit unless you remain in me. I am the vine; you are the branches. If you remain in me and I in you, you will bear much fruit; apart from me you can do nothing." In Christ, my daughter and son-in-law are connected to the Vine, the Author and Finisher of their faith. They have access to everything they need. Please bless them with the desire and resolve to remain in You. Remind them that apart from You they cannot experience peace or do anything of eternal or earthly value or significance.

Lord, most of the time we don't recognize our need for peace until we find ourselves in difficult, confusing, or frustrating circumstances. When trials come that are beyond our ability to control or handle, we sometimes search for a quick way out. Peace also seems elusive when the situation necessitates waiting. Father, before my daughter and son-in-law choose to react, please remind them to seek You first. While they wait for Your peace, give them clarity and direction. Help them to discern Your voice above the others that would distract them from Your purpose.

Father, we can become impatient and lack peace because we don't get what we want when we want it. Lord, what _____ and _____ want is not always what they need. Please give them wisdom to know the difference. Help them to trust and believe that You to know exactly what they need; remind them that You've promised to faithfully supply everything they need for life and godliness. In Christ, they lack nothing. Help them to be at peace in every circumstance because they trust You to take care of every spoken and unspoken need they have.

Lord, there may be times when _____ and _____ have prayed faithfully and repeatedly about something, and yet it may seem their prayers go unanswered. Remind them that You are always at work on their behalf, even when they don't see You move. Help them to be still and know that You are God (Psalm 46:10). You are listening, and their prayers matter to You. Lord, please blanket them with Your perfect peace; encourage them as they wait patiently for Your answer. And if the answer they receive is not what they had hoped and prayed for, please comfort them, Lord. Please help them to be "joyful in hope, patient in affliction, faithful in prayer" (Romans 12:12), and to trust and persevere no matter what.

Father, my daughter and future son-in-law have so much to do and lots of decisions to make before the wedding. Please help them to walk in peace and be patient with each other, bearing in mind that not only are peace and patience fruit of the Spirit, but an expression of love as well. Please help them to extend this kind of love toward each other and everyone else they interact with as they continue planning for the wedding. Lord, please keep them in perfect peace; help their minds to remain steadfast and focused on You. Heavenly Father, with all they have going on right now, please keep their hearts from being troubled. Help them to rest in the peace You have already provided for them through Christ. Thank You, Lord!

In Jesus's name, amen.

. . . .

For God is not a God of disorder but of peace.
1 CORINTHIANS 14:33

Challenge #6

I'm just wondering. Do you text, or would you rather talk on the phone? Maybe you like to email or message people through social media. Or maybe you're like me, and you use all of the above to communicate.

Not too long ago, my mom called me. We talk, or rather text, all the time, so I was surprised and immediately answered the phone. Because we usually text, I was concerned and thought something was wrong. Thank God, nothing was wrong, and all she wanted was to hear my voice. *All she wanted was to hear my voice.* Makes me get a bit emotional just thinking about it. Although nothing was wrong when my mom called me that day, there was a lot that wasn't right.

We live in a technology saturated and addicted world. I'm sure this is no surprise to you. If you're a parent, you know what I am talking about. While technology clearly provides a lot of good, the bad tends to outweigh the benefits. For the sake of who knows what, we are losing the ability and joy of communicating with each other. Having simple or heart-to-heart conversations over the phone—or in person for that matter—is far from the norm these days. To be honest, I text way more than I talk, and it is not okay. It's sad and unhealthy.

This brings me to your final challenge. Will you consider making some phone calls today to people you haven't spoken to lately or people you have only communicated with through text or messaging? Okay, maybe you're buried in bride business; I understand completely. If today doesn't work, please find another day and time. I don't want you to miss out on the blessings wrapped up in this challenge. Of all the challenges I have encouraged you to participate in, this one is by far the most important. Why? Because the people in your life are important. They matter to God, and they matter to you.

So please take the challenge and decide right now who you will call. Maybe it's your mom and dad, or brother or sister, or your best friend from high school. When you make time to do what you don't normally do, it matters. If you usually text, make a phone call. If you usually talk on the phone, maybe buy a card and send it in the mail. Try to do something that you don't normally do. Lastly, enjoy every minute of this challenge, and maybe the next time you go to text, email, or message on Facebook, you'll make the call instead. God bless you!

veryone you know who's been in a wedding or gotten married has probably already told you this, but please let me add my voice: "It will go by faster than you think—all the planning and especially the wedding day." Whether you have a few months or more than a year to plan for the big day, I promise you, it will be here before you know it. Like me, you'll soon be looking back, reminiscing, and wishing you could do it all over again. I even miss the not-so-much-fun parts and the tears because every moment meant something special. It was all part of the process of God preparing my daughter's heart for her wedding. And it was all worth it—the good, the bad, and the ugly.

I feel like I could probably write a book on wedding tips, but I think that, other than prayer, this final tip is the most valuable and significant. Make it your job, in all the planning and preparation, to capture the memories. You'll have lots of opportunities to do so. Of course, picking out table linens and wedding cake flavors might not be all that memorable or exciting (unless you get to taste the cake), but doing it together is.

God willing, your daughter's wedding is a once-in-a-lifetime celebration. You won't get to spend time with her like this ever again. You will only get to witness the expression on her face when she tries on *the dress* once. You will help her design her wedding invitations once. These moments are fleeting. So my final suggestion or tip is that, for as many days and moments that you have the privilege to help your daughter plan and prepare for her wedding, you become a *mommarazzi*.

What exactly is a mommarazzi, you ask? Well, I am one, so I can tell you everything I know.

It's being there for every moment possible, and in the midst of them, capturing everything you can. It's about being present for all the little moments, and while you're there, taking pictures, grabbing business cards, brochures, receipts—anything and everything that will represent the moment, because eventually, that moment will become a memory. No matter what part of the planning process we were in the middle of, I documented everything. Yes, I was a bit zealous at times . . . but it was all worth it.

In addition to taking pictures and grabbing mementoes, I wrote everything down. This is where you get creative. During the wedding planning process, I stored the mementoes and pictures in a journal and then I wrote about the experience—what I saw, how I felt, and everything about Erin that I could possibly write. I did this because I wanted to have an account of everything, and pictures and brochures and mementoes can only tell you so much. I decided to take the time (and trust me, it takes time) to write about it. And what a treasure the end result is.

After compiling everything in a journal, I gave the journal to Erin as a gift—an account of her wedding planning journey. A gift she will have for the rest of her life; a gift she can go back to and look at to be reminded of how God blessed her through all the details. It's a gift that she can someday share with her daughter as she plans for her wedding.

I'm telling you, I blew up my phone with hundreds of photos . . . I had a drawer overflowing with more wedding stuff than you could possibly think of . . . but it was all worth it.

Take this tip to heart, my friend. You and your daughter will be so thankful and blessed that you did.

(Quick note: The next few prayers are specific to the actual wedding day. Depending on what time the wedding ceremony is, you might want to read these the night before, or a few days before the wedding. It's up to you. Can you believe the big day is finally here? I'm so excited for you and your daughter. I'm praying for you.)

Father God,

Wow! It's hard to believe that today is my daughter's wedding day. Wasn't it just a minute ago that she got engaged and we started planning? It seems like yesterday I was cradling her in my arms, close to my chest, rocking her to sleep. Where did the time go?

Lord, You have been with us all along. You have watched over our coming and going and carried us through every storm and heartbreak. You have blessed us beyond measure and cheered with us during every accomplishment and triumph. From day one, You have been with us and for us, faithfully and sovereignly orchestrating every detail of our lives for Your glory and our good. And now here we are. *Your* daughter is getting married. She is sacrificially, wholeheartedly giving her life to her husband today, the man You chose for her to marry before the creation of the world.

I'm overcome with thanksgiving and joy. I stand in awe of You today, Lord—in awe of Your love, forgiveness, mercy, and grace. For the countless ways You have provided for _____ and protected her heart. She is Yours! You are her first love. Thank You for blessing her with the desire to know and love You more. Thank You for placing Your Holy Spirit in her, and filling her with the fruit of the Spirit. Thank You for beginning a good work in her life, a good work that You have promised to faithfully complete. You are amazing! You are so generous and kind.

Lord, thank You for bringing my husband and me together at just the right time and for blessing us with the gift of children. Thank You for choosing me to be _____'s mother. She is a treasure to our family and a gift to all who know her. Lord, thank You for filling us with Your love so that we can love each other and others like You do. Father, I love my daughter so much, and yet I know that You love her more, with a perfect love that is far beyond my ability to comprehend.

Thank You for the gift of _____'s life. What an honor and privilege it has been to be her mother. Thank You for giving me the awesome responsibility to raise and teach her all that I know. Although I have fallen short more times than I can count, I trust that You have allowed her to learn and grow from my mistakes. Thank You, heavenly Father.

Thank You for allowing me to comfort _____ during seasons of heartbreak and rejoice with her during seasons of triumph. Thank You for every moment we have been able to spend together. What a gift it has been to laugh and cry with her. And what a blessing it has been to help her prepare for her wedding day. Thank You, Lord!

As I prepare to be the mother of the bride today, please ready my heart and mind. It's not about me—everything about this day is about You, and the beauty and holiness of what You will do in and through my daughter and her groom as they pledge their commitment and love for each other. Father, more than anything, I long to extend the love and grace that You have given me to everyone, throughout the entire day.

From getting dressed and ready with the girls, to the moment when our last guest leaves for the night, please allow me to be a blessing and to radiate Your glory. Father, search my heart and show me if there is any offensive way in me, so that I can repent and receive Your forgiveness. Lord, I pray that every time I open my mouth, words of love and encouragement would pour out. If something goes wrong today, please help me to respond in prayer and to remain calm and trust that You will take care of everything.

This is the day the Lord has made, I will rejoice and be glad! Thank You, Father, for who You are and all that You have done on our behalf. As You have so abundantly blessed us, I pray that today's wedding of _____ and _____ would bless You.

In Jesus's awesome name I pray, amen.

. . . .

May the God of endurance and encouragement grant you
to live in such harmony with one another, in accord with Christ Jesus,
that together you may with one voice glorify the God
and Father of our Lord Jesus Christ.
ROMANS 15:5–6 ESV

Her children arise and call her blessed;
her husband also, and he praises her.
PROVERBS 31:28

THE GROOM

Father,

Thank You, Lord! You are such a good Father and have graciously orchestrated every moment and every detail leading up to the wedding day. We have been anticipating and looking forward to this celebration of love and commitment with great joy and excitement. We have planned and prayed, laughed and cried, and today everything will come to fruition. Thank You for this amazing, life-changing day. Thank You for preparing _____ and _____ in advance to walk into the covenant of marriage—a covenant that You created to express Your unconditional love and faithfulness.

My heart is overwhelmed with gratitude for all that You have done thus far and all that You will continue to do from this day forward. You are God, and there is none like You. Before You knit my daughter together in my womb, You knew that she would be the one for _____ and he would be the one for her. He was Your choice before he was my daughter's choice. And before he becomes my daughter's husband and our son-in-law, it is comforting to rest in the reality that he has always been Yours. Your child. Your creation. Your chosen vessel to display Your glory upon the earth. Lord, thank You for choosing him to be Your very own. For creating him on purpose for a purpose!

Heavenly Father, please meet with _____ today as he gets ready to meet his bride at the altar. He probably has a lot on his mind and heart. I am so thankful that You know exactly what he is thinking and feeling in these moments. If he is anxious about anything, please flood him with Your peace. Supply every need he has right now so that he can walk into this covenant with complete confidence and joy.

As _____ puts on his wedding day outfit, please dress him in the armor of God: the helmet of salvation to protect his mind—in You he has the mind of Christ; the breastplate of righteousness to protect his heart—Father, create in him a pure and contrite heart; the belt of truth buckled around his waist—please protect him from the enemy's lies! Lord, grant him the strength to resist compromise and give him a heartfelt passion to listen to the voice of truth. Lord, in addition to all this, please prepare him with the shield of faith that extinguishes all the flaming arrows of the evil one, and the sword of the Spirit which is the Word of God. Please hide Your Word in his heart so that he will not sin against You. And lastly, Lord, please prepare _____'s feet to take the gospel wherever you call him (Ephesians 6:10–17). Thank You, Lord!

Father, thank You for my daughter's soon-to-be husband. Thank You for bringing him into her life at just the right time, for such a time as this. Lord, I pray that just as Jesus loves the church, His bride, this beloved man will love Your precious daughter. You have heard every prayer I have prayed; You have answered my prayers in Your perfect way and timing. Lord, I praise You for Your sovereignty and love. I do not have to worry or be anxious about what lies ahead for them, because You're already there orchestrating every detail for Your glory and their good.

Lord, thank You in advance for all that You will do in and through the wedding couple today. I pray that You would do immeasurably more than I could ever pray or imagine. Lord, make Your powerful presence throughout the day unmistakable. Allow the radiance of Your glory to rest upon _____ and _____ in such a profound and mighty way that they would not only remember this day because it is their wedding day, but because of Your hand upon their lives. Thank You for Your perfect, unconditional love. Thank You for the gift of marriage. Jesus, You are, always have been, and always will be the greatest gift!

In Your mighty name, I pray, amen.

Therefore what God has joined together, let no one separate.
MARK 10:9

Dear God,

I am so grateful for the amazing people that my family and I have been blessed to share our lives with. Thank You for handpicking every person that we get to call our family and friends. There are acquaintances and guests whom we've invited to the wedding, and then there are those in our family and inner circle—the ones we are closest to. They've seen the good, the bad, the ugly; they've been here through the ups and the downs, the trials and triumphs, and still, they love and accept us without reservation. It is such a joy to share this day with them as we celebrate this pivotal moment: _____ and _____'s wedding day.

To have our immediate family members and close friends be a part of this life-changing event means so much to us. You have purposely brought these people into our lives, Lord, so I ask that You would return to them a hundredfold the countless blessings they have poured into our lives.

I pray, God, that each of these people would see and marvel at the majesty of Your love and power as it resonates through_____ and her fiancé, _____. As they commit their lives to one another, please bless those who mean so much to us with unprecedented joy. During the ceremony and reception and while we are all together during the wedding weekend, please give our family members and this intimate circle of friends eyes to see and ears to hear. Fill them with everlasting joy and hope. Encourage and inspire them, young and old, with all You have accomplished thus far, in and through my daughter and her fiancé's relationship. Please let them see the limitless possibilities for their own lives; show our friends and family through this wedding couple's example what it looks like to seek after You and follow You wholeheartedly, passionately, and unreservedly.

Father, I ask that as family and friends observe the undeniable love You have for _____ and _____ and the deep abiding love they have for each other—that they too would become acutely aware of Your love and presence. Stir a hunger for You and Your will in their lives as they see my daughter and her future husband so completely fulfilled in their love for You.

Father, You are the author of relationships. You created and designed us to need You and each other. Lord, some of our family members and friends do not have a relationship with You. Not only do some of them not know You, they do not have good family relationships and friendships either. Would You help these people admit their need, seek a relationship with You, and as a result, discover that You heal the brokenhearted and save those who are crushed in spirit? Would You break down walls that have caused division and separation? Father, would You please heal and mend broken relationships? Would You help our family members and friends who have unresolved issues that need to be addressed? Lord, please restore and protect the relationships You have ordained.

Heavenly Father, I further pray that our family members and friends would see Your joy in and through my daughter and son-in-law. That they would want what _____ and _____ have found in Christ: Your peace, Your love, Your redemption, Your will, Your favor—and so much more.

I pray that as close as we all are in this inner circle, that through this beautiful experience, we would grow closer and find a deeper appreciation for each other and the relationships You have given us.

In Jesus's name I pray, amen.

. . . .

A friend loves at all times.

PROVERBS 17:17

Father,

It is an incredible blessing to have our friends and family come together to celebrate _____ and _____ and to share such a meaningful day with us. Each person that we've invited to this once-in-a-lifetime celebration of love and commitment is important to us and was thoughtfully and intentionally chosen. Best of all, Lord, You have handpicked everyone that You want to be here. I am so thankful. God, I pray that You would bless our guests beyond measure and that the meaning of love and marriage would touch them deeply and refresh their lives.

Lord, from the moment our guests arrive, I pray they would be treated like and feel like royalty. May Your Spirit move at the wedding ceremony and reception so that everyone will feel loved and appreciated. Lord, would You please extend Your favor upon this celebration of marriage in such a profound manner that every person would experience Your power, presence, and perfect love. Let a deep, abiding, and undeniable awareness of something more—something eternal, something godly—settle upon them.

Please use the wedding ceremony and reception to reveal Your favor, goodness, and beauty. There will be guests in attendance who do not know You as Savior and Lord, so I pray that Your love and purpose here today would be undeniable for them. In fact, I am asking that our guests would leave this celebration forever changed and longing for more. Yes, Lord, I pray that Your presence would so permeate every aspect of the wedding that people's lives will be dramatically changed. Only You can do this!

For married couples in attendance who are struggling to survive or for those on the verge of giving up, please intervene. Give them hope, healing, patience, and understanding. As _____ and _____ profess their love and commitment to each other, I pray that all who are married would be refreshed and encouraged. Ignite a fire in their hearts, Lord, that lights the path to a deeper love for You and each other in a way they have not experienced before.

Father, from the smallest, unnoticeable details to the most important aspects of the ceremony and reception, would You please allow everything to flow effortlessly, so that Your hand is evident in all things? If You are involved, I know this will be an unforgettable experience.

O Lord, as far as food, travel, accommodations, and all the other details concerning our guests, I pray that all would go smoothly—that flights would be on time and hotel rooms would be clean and ready. You've created delicious food for us to enjoy, so, Father, I pray that even the food, from presentation to taste, would display Your glory. From the rehearsal dinner, cocktail hour, grand reception, and even to the morning-after brunch—may it all reflect Your favor and blessing. Lord, regarding all the specifics of the music and entertainment, I pray that it would honor You while also blessing our guests.

Lord, keep evil from disrupting or destroying any part of this event. Keep drunkenness or any other unclean actions, attitudes, or substances away from the wedding celebration. Please help our guests be respectful and responsible. Keep them from overindulging so that nothing would take away from the beauty and holiness of the day.

Father, I pray for every single person involved in making this wedding and reception a success—from those who entertain, drive, and clean to those who cook, coordinate, and manage. Lord, bless every person involved in the complex, countless details necessary to make this celebration unforgettable. I also pray that the staff and vendors would personally be filled with Your wisdom, patience, and favor. As a result of being involved in the wedding (even if they do not know or acknowledge You), I pray that they would have the desire and motivation to serve You, and would thereby bless our guests and the bride and groom with joyful, competent service.

I truly believe that this wedding is bigger than two people coming together to pledge their love and commitment, bigger than two families uniting; this wedding is a witness to the reality of who You are, Lord. It's about You . . . Your power, Your purpose, and Your love.

Thank You for hearing my prayer and for allowing us to witness and participate in _____ and _____'s wedding day. I pray that it will be unforgettable and that every person will leave closer to You than they were when they arrived.

In Jesus's name I pray, amen.

. . . .

Whether you eat or drink or whatever you do,
do it all for the glory of God.
1 CORINTHIANS 10:31

Serve wholeheartedly,
as if you were serving the Lord, not people.
EPHESIANS 6:7

FROM THIS DAY FORWARD

Father God,

When the wedding ceremony and celebration come to an end, You remain. When _____ and _____ begin their new life together as husband and wife, Your presence goes with them. You will never leave them nor forsake them. As You have from the beginning, You will continue to provide for every need _____ and _____ have from this day forward. You are a covenant maker and keeper. Your love, promises, and faithfulness endure forever, and Your mercies are new every morning. Thank You, Lord!

From this day forward, life will be filled with challenges and changes. But You remain the same, yesterday, today, and forever (Hebrews 13:8). You never change. Lord, nothing surprises You or throws You off guard. From joy-filled victories to seasons of waiting and heartbreak and every moment in between—You are God. Whenever _____ and _____ grow weary or burdened, help them to come to You for encouragement and rest (Matthew 11:28–30). You know the number of days You've ordained for them; You've planned in advance the good works they will walk into as a married couple. When fear of the unknown tempts _____ and _____ to be anxious or worried about the future, please remind them to walk by faith, not by sight. Please strengthen them according to Your Word, Lord.

Heavenly Father, from this day forward, _____ and _____ have a lot to learn and, God willing, a whole lot of living to do. Help them be obedient to Your will and never let them lose sight of the purpose for which they have been created and called. Teach _____ and _____ to commit everything to You and to choose what is right, simply because it's the right thing to do. Lord, please help them focus on and delight only in what is true, noble, praiseworthy, and excellent. When _____ and _____ are tempted to conform to the pattern of this world, remind them to pray immediately. Father, please renew their minds and help them trust You to take care of everything in Your perfect way and timing.

Lord, from this day forward, please remind _____ and _____ that their lives are but a breath. Teach them to number their days that they may gain hearts filled with wisdom. Father, remind them that they did not choose You but that You chose them and appointed them to bear fruit that will last (John 15:16). Help them to acknowledge You and always remember that apart from You, they can do nothing (John 15:5). Please hide Your Word in their hearts and help them to put it into daily practice. When _____ and _____ fall short, remind them that Jesus and the Holy Spirit intercede for them at all times. Thank You, Father!

God, from this day forward, I pray that _____ and _____ would never get over You. Help them grow more in awe of Your sovereignty, holiness, and power every day. Captivate them with Your love, grace, forgiveness, and mercy all the days of their lives. Father, please help _____ and _____ to wholeheartedly pursue You so they can know and love You more and love others unconditionally. Rather than earthly gain, inspire them to store up heavenly treasures that will never perish, spoil, or fade. Lord, please prove their faith genuine and prepare them one day at a time, one prayer at a time, to meet You face to face. Thank You for hearing my prayers and answering them according to Your glory and perfect will. You are amazing!

In Jesus's awesome name, amen.

. . . .

In their hearts, humans plan their course,
but the LORD establishes their steps.
PROVERBS 16:9

Epilogue

*I*n two days my husband and I will celebrate six months of marriage. I am more in love with him today than I ever thought possible. It's as if every day that goes by God is molding our hearts so that our love for each other looks more like His love.

The last six months have been amazing, but far from easy. After our incredible wedding, Parker and I entered into a season filled with one trial after another, including my father being diagnosed for the third time with squamous cell carcinoma—oral cancer of the upper jaw. We spent the entire fourth month of our marriage in a hospital room in New York City, while my father underwent facial reconstruction surgery. As difficult as this season was, Parker and I learned more about each other than we could have ever imagined. We learned to depend on God and as a result we began to depend on and love each other more. I was able to experience immeasurable joy as a result of watching my husband take care of my father.

In the midst of the pain of those months, joy and love prevailed and grew. Because our foundation was rooted in love, faithfulness, and prayer, Parker and I still found joy through this season of our life. We are so thankful for every moment, every tear, every smile, and every "I love you" that has brought us to this day. And the truth is, it all started with prayer: prayers for my husband that were written when I was just a little girl; prayers since my engagement that God would prepare my heart to become Parker's wife;

Parker's prayers to be a godly and loving husband and the same for me as his wife; prayers that people would see Jesus throughout our wedding day, that they would see the love of Christ in the way Parker and I love each other; my parents' prayers throughout my entire life; my mother's prayers as we planned for the wedding; our prayers together, as mother and daughter, longing for God to be glorified and honored through both of our marriages; prayers that have shaped who I am and changed the trajectory of my life. It all started with prayer.

My prayer for you is that you walk away from this book more in love with Jesus and your future husband than you ever thought you could be. That you are fully equipped and ready to commit your heart and life on your wedding day. That no matter what happens from your wedding day forward, you will be reminded of the faithfulness of God and the prayers you prayed in this book. That you would have a deeper relationship with Christ and an even closer relationship with your mother as a result of sharing this prayer journey.

I challenge you to continue to pray. Continue to ask God to strengthen your marriage and love. Pray for any future children. And I pray that you and your husband would love and pray like Jesus. That God would guard and protect what He has brought together. I pray that you and your husband would pray for each other daily.

Pray without ceasing—because your wedding is just the beginning.

Erin

With Gratitude

When it comes to raising children in the twenty-first century (or any century for that matter), it has often been said, "It takes a village!" It takes the same to put a book like this in your hands. The "village" that God so graciously assembled for such a time as this was exactly who we needed to bless you as you journey through wedding planning and preparation.

A little behind-the-scenes action for you . . .

During the editing process, Erin and I had a lot going on—we were planning her wedding, she got married, went on her honeymoon; soon after they returned from their honeymoon, Erin's husband, Parker, was released from the minor league baseball team he'd been pitching for . . . and my husband, Jim, was diagnosed with squamous cell carcinoma (oral cancer) for the third time.

To say that we had our hands full would be a gross understatement. So we called in the village—and everyone who stepped in played a vital role in making this book a reality and a blessing.

FROM JILL & ERIN

King of kings, Prince of Peace, Everlasting Father . . . Lord Jesus—"Thank You" always seems inadequate, and yet words and hearts full of gratitude and praise are what we have to offer. Without You, our hearts are empty, life is meaningless, and everything we have to give is insignificant. You are and will always be *everything*. We have no idea why You would choose to use the two of us to write this book, but we are so thankful that You did. Thank You for every word, every struggle, every mountain, every valley it took to get here. We trust You to use it all for Your glory and kingdom. We love You!

Rick Kern—Here we are again. God has allowed us to partner for another amazing book. In the midst of this journey, you had your own mountain to climb, and yet, as you always do, you remained faithful and steadfast. As we've said in the past, we would never want to write anything without you. You are a gifted writer and editor extraordinaire. We continue to learn so much from you. But it's your love for Jesus that has taught us the most. Thank you, Rick . . . our dear friend, brother, mentor, and burn-the-midnight-oil editor.

Natalie Hanemann—You're right, it is no coincidence that the Lord paired us together for this project. You had to put up with a lot, and you did it so graciously. Although we have never met face-to-face and we know so little about each other, God has blessed us with a heart connection we will cherish forever. Thank you for editing and for everything, but especially for the spirit of gentleness in which you handled all that we went through during the writing of this book. None of this would have come to fruition without you. You are a gift, and you are gifted. We are so grateful that God chose to use you to craft this book into exactly what He wanted it to be. Well done!

Jana Burson—Thank you, yet again, for believing in the heart and purpose of this book. It has always been and will always be a blessing and a privilege to have you as our literary agent extraordinaire. However, the greater gift is your love and friendship. If we lived closer to each other, hanging out would be a once-a-week kind of thing. We love you so much and cannot thank you enough for being there for our family beyond the context of book writing. You're a blessing! And *Go Bills*!

Marilyn Jansen and the entire Worthy Publishing Group team— Wow! With all that our family had going on during the writing of this book, we thought for sure you might throw in the towel. But you didn't. Like Natalie, you extended great patience and kindness toward us. You prayed for and encouraged us to persevere. And persevere we did. Thank you for being so excited and committed to making this book a reality. Thank you for sticking with us and standing by our family. God is going to use the words and prayers on these pages in a mighty, powerful way. Thank you for making our heartfelt vision for brides and their mothers into a reading reality. We've loved working with you and hope this is the first of many future endeavors.

Grammie—God gave us the vision and the words for this book, but He also gave us you, your encouragement, and your prayers. Thank you for loving us and taking care of us. There is no one on the planet that either of us would want to be like and emulate more than you. Your love for Jesus and His Word is the greatest gift God has given us through your amazing life. We thank God for you and love you *so much*!

FROM JILL TO ERIN MARIE

Words fall short. As your mother, I am amazed by how God continues to mold and shape you into the woman of God He desires. You are more like Jesus than anyone I know (you and Grammie). I will never forget the wise advice you gave me as we wrote: "Mom, just pray. Don't write. Pray!" Thank you for always being patient and kind to me, Erin. I'm not kidding when I say I want to be more like you. You were a beautiful bride, and your insight and prayers will be invaluable to every bride who reads this book. I'm proud of you, and I love you more than you will ever know.

FROM ERIN TO JILL

Mom, here we are, at the end of writing our second book together. What a tremendous honor it is to write alongside you! You are and always will be my best friend. You are the most incredible woman I know. Thank you for constantly pointing me to Jesus. I know more of God's love because of your love for me and for our family. Thank you for all you did to make my wedding day the best day of my life. You were the most stunning mother of the bride! Thank you for consistently teaching me about love, forgiveness, and Jesus. I hope and pray that one day I will be a mother like you. I love you . . . more. Always more.

FROM ERIN TO PARKER

Parker Bean . . . my husband, best friend, love of my life . . . you are the answer to my prayer. You are immeasurably more than all I could have ever asked God for. I know more of God's love because of the way you love me. I'm so thankful that God chose YOU to be my forever. I love you . . . more and more every single day!

About the Authors

JILL KELLY is a *New York Times* best-selling author, event speaker, and the wife of retired Buffalo Bills quarterback and pro football hall of famer Jim Kelly. Jill and Jim have three children—Erin, twenty-three years old; Hunter (February 14, 1997–August 5, 2005); and Camryn, nineteen years old. As founder and chairman of the board of Hunter's Hope Foundation, Jill helps children with Krabbe leukodystrophy and their families by extending the hope and comfort she has received through her relationship with Christ.

ERIN KELLY-BEAN is a *New York Times* best-selling author, event speaker, and the oldest daughter of Jill Kelly and her husband, retired Buffalo Bills quarterback and pro football hall of famer Jim Kelly. Erin has an inter-disciplinary degree in digital media and strategic communications from Liberty University. She is currently attending Liberty University School of Law. Erin is a member of the board for Hunter's Hope Foundation. She lives with her husband, Parker, and their dog, Blu, in Lynchburg, Virginia.

IF YOU ENJOYED THIS BOOK, WILL YOU CONSIDER SHARING THE MESSAGE WITH OTHERS?

Mention the book in a blog post or through Facebook, Twitter, Pinterest, or upload a picture through Instagram.

Recommend this book to those in your small group, book club, workplace, and classes.

Head over to facebook.com/worthypublishing, "LIKE" the page, and post a comment as to what you enjoyed the most.

Pick up a copy for someone you know who would be challenged and encouraged by this message.

Write a book review online.

WORTHY®
PUBLISHING

Visit us at worthypublishing.com

twitter.com/worthypub

worthypub.tumblr.com

facebook.com/worthypublishing

pinterest.com/worthypub

instagram.com/worthypub

youtube.com/worthypublishing